When Your
Rope Breaks

Other Books by Steve Brown

Born Free: How to Find Radical Freedom and Infectious Joy in Authentic Faith (plus study guide)

Living Free: How to Live a Life of Radical Freedom and Infectious Joy (plus study guide)

How to Talk So People Will Listen

If God Is in Charge: Thoughts on the Nature of God for Skeptics, Christians, and Skeptical Christians

If Jesus Has Come: Thoughts on the Incarnation for Skeptics, Christians, and Skeptical Christians

When Being Good Isn't Good Enough

When Your Rope Breaks

Steve Brown

A Raven's Ridge Book

 **BakerBooks**

A Division of Baker Book House Co.
Grand Rapids, Michigan 49516

©1988 by Stephen W. Brown

Published by Raven's Ridge Books
an imprint of Baker Book House Company
P.O. Box 6287, Grand Rapids, MI 49516-6287

Paperback edition published 1996
Fourth printing, November 2001

Previously published by Thomas Nelson, Inc., Publishers

Printed in the United States of America

Library of Congress Cataloging-in-Publication Data

Brown, Stephen W.
    When your rope breaks / Steve Brown.
      p. cm.
    Originally published : Nashville : T. Nelson, c1988.
    "A Raven's Ridge book."
    Includes bibliographical references.
    ISBN 0-8010-5729-9 (paper)
      1. Consolation. 2. Encouragement—Religious aspects—
Christianity. I. Title
BV4905.2.B73 1996
248.8'6—dc20   96-18304

For current information about all releases available from Baker Book House, visit our web site:
                  http://www.bakerbooks.com/

In memory
of
Matthew Asher
"A happy gift of God"

Since you were precious in My sight, you have been honored, and I have loved you.

Isaiah 43:4 NKJV

CONTENTS

ACKNOWLEDGMENTS

The Acknowledgments of a book is a lot like a committee . . . an effort to spread the blame.

My thanks to those, who for better or worse, contributed to this book:

Vic Oliver, whose wise counsel and tight rein kept my "good stuff" from becoming an embarrassment . . .

Susan Salmon, whose significant gifts at editing made this book far more readable than it would have been . . .

Cathy Wyatt, who always makes what I do better . . .

My wife, Anna, who reads me and my manuscripts with more discernment than anyone I know . . .

Our daughter Robin, who took the time to add her writing skills to mine . . .

Our daughter Jennifer, who is the consummate "cheerleader" from her dorm room at college . . .

And to the people of the Key Biscayne Presbyterian Church whose lives are living illustrations of what is taught in this book.

I suspect I have left out many who have contributed to this book.

Some of them are grateful.

1

The Bad News

Why is light given to a man whose way is hidden,
And whom God has hedged in?
For my sighing comes before I eat,
And my groanings pour out like water.
For the thing I greatly feared has come upon me,
And what I dreaded has happened to me.
I am not at ease, nor am I quiet;
I have no rest, for trouble comes.

Job 3:23–26

I was watching the news when a picture of a hotel fire in Puerto Rico flashed on the screen. People were screaming, climbing out of windows onto flimsy ropes, hoping to get to safety. As I heard their screams and saw the flames threatening to engulf them, I put myself in their place and vicariously experienced their panic and the panic of those who were trying desperately to quench the fire.

I'll bet there was a similar thought in the minds of every person trying to escape. They were all wondering, *What is going to happen if the rope breaks?*

Most of us are familiar with that type of situation, with the painful wondering, *What if the rope breaks?* That is what this book is all about—Broken Rope Syndrome (BRS). In the following pages we are going to be talking about what it is and how Christians deal with it.

9

Have you ever read a book on how to make your prayer life more effective and put the principles into practice, only to find that God seemed to have gone away on vacation to Bermuda? Have you ever practiced someone's five principles for a happy marriage and found that your marriage became worse? Have you ever listened to a sermon on how to handle temptation, followed the advice, and found that the temptation turned into sin?

Perhaps you claimed God's promises for healing and found that you were still sick. Or obeyed the ten commandments for parents, only to discover that your teenager was on drugs. Have you suffered and not learned anything from it? Have you faced the death of someone you loved and not been able to find meaning in it?

If you have experienced any of the above, then you are a victim of BRS. And if you are a victim, then this book is for you. Most books tell you how to make things better. In this book I want to talk to those who have tried everything and it still isn't better.

"I followed all the biblical principles," the businessman said, shifting uncomfortably in the chair across from my desk. "I only hired Christians; we had prayer in my office every morning; I used my business as a witness for Christ. And now it's all coming apart. I don't mind so much for myself, but I am very worried about my witness. I told all of my friends that this was a Christian business, and because it was Christian, God would honor it. What will they think about Christ?"

Almost every day I hear another story of someone who did everything right yet found that everything had gone wrong. We don't talk much about the subject, but it's an important one. I want to share with you my twenty-five years of experience as a pastor, in which I have been asking the questions related to BRS. I think I've found some answers—not glib, easy, shallow answers, but answers that will do until we get home to heaven.

God is sovereign. He is good and He knows what He is doing. That's the good news. Try to remember that for a chapter or two, because we're going to wade through a lot of mud before we find some diamonds from the Father.

All Is Not Right with the World

Long before we were born something bad happened called the Fall, and today we are dealing with the repercussions. Adam and Eve, our first parents, disobeyed God's instructions in the Garden. I don't think it's fair, but because they made such a mess of it, we have to suffer.

Of course, no one asked me.

As a result of the Fall, we must face a number of facts that make most people uncomfortable and that most people don't like to consider. When all of the systems work for you—when your prayers are answered as you would like and you can say with Robert Browning, "God's in his heaven—All's right with the world!"—you don't have to deal with the unpleasant facts.

When the rope has broken and you have fallen in the dirt, however, it is perhaps an appropriate time to examine the dirt—to study your circumstances. If you are a victim of BRS, you can't afford to close your eyes and pretend that everything is fine. You must look at the facts without clichés, pious platitudes, and the silly, colored glasses of Pollyanna. If there is anything good about falling in the dirt (and there is precious little) it is that your situation quickly forces you to get honest. Dirt is something most of us would rather ignore. But when you are in it, it's very hard to miss.

The Inevitable Storms in a Fallen World

First, because of the Fall, we live in a physical world where something is terribly wrong. Not only do people suffer as a result of Adam and Eve's disobedience but the earth also suffers.

After the Fall, God told Adam and Eve they were responsible human beings who must now face the repercussions of their disobedience. God said to Eve, "I will greatly multiply your sorrow and your conception; In pain you shall bring forth children" (Gen. 3:16). God said to Adam,

> *"Cursed is the ground for your sake;*
> *In toil you shall eat of it*
> *All the days of your life.*
> *Both thorns and thistles it shall bring forth for you,*
> *And you shall eat the herb of the field.*
> *In the sweat of your face you shall eat bread*
> *Till you return to the ground,*
> *For out of it you were taken;*
> *For dust you are,*
> *And to dust you shall return."*
>
> *(Gen. 3:17b–19)*

In the New Testament, Paul wrote about the repercussions the physical world bore because of the Fall: "For
the creation was subjected to futility, not willingly, but
because of Him who subjected it in hope. . . . For we
know that the whole creation groans and labors with
birth pangs together until now" (Rom. 8:20–22).

As I was leaving to speak at a family conference in
the mountains of Pennsylvania, I found myself under
heavy pressure because I had heard a hurricane was ap-
proaching my home in Miami. Before I left, I called our
local weather forecasters and asked them the odds of the
hurricane's reaching South Florida. Although no one
could predict for sure, they felt certain that it would skirt
the southern tip of Florida and enter the Gulf. With those
words of comfort, I flew to Pennsylvania.

As soon as I got to the conference grounds, I turned
on the radio to find that my sources had made a serious
mistake. The hurricane was headed right for my house.
The airports were closed, and I couldn't fly back home.

I don't know about you, but I verbalize my anxiety.
Every time I got up to speak, I said something about being worried about my family. Also, each time I spoke I
noticed a small group of people in the back of the auditorium, gathered in a huddle. I sometimes wondered what
they were doing, but it was a rather free group of people
and whatever they were doing was O.K.

Between sessions, I phoned my wife and daughters
and told them to "batten down the hatches" of our home
and drive immediately to Orlando to stay with some
friends who lived there. After they finally arrived in Orlando (in the middle of the state) I felt relieved that they
were out of danger.

Do you know what happened? That hurricane missed Miami altogether. In fact, it came right up to the coast and then, for some strange reason, turned north. I announced the good news to the people at the conference.

After I had finished speaking a young man came up to me and said, "Mr. Brown, did you notice that whenever you were speaking a group of us were gathered in the back of the auditorium?" I allowed that I had noticed. "Do you know what we were doing?" he asked. "We were praying that hurricane away from Miami. It turned north because we asked the Lord to turn it north."

To this day I am not sure if the hurricane changed course because of their prayers or because of the weather front which moved in from the west. Maybe it was a combination of both or maybe neither.

However, the irony of the episode was that when it became clear that the hurricane was not going to hit Miami, my family began the drive back to South Florida. About that time the hurricane turned west again and swept across the state, catching my family in the middle of their drive back home. Everyone was O.K., but it was a harrowing experience.

What's the point? Just this: Hurricanes are inevitable in a fallen world. Things are bent and wrong, and the Bible says they won't be put right until Jesus comes again. I'm not sure the people in Central Florida would have been very pleased with the folks who prayed the hurricane away from Miami and onto their shores. Perhaps, if they had known how to pray, they could have sent it to Georgia. At any rate, someone would have had to deal with that hurricane because hurricanes are a part of a fallen world.

If you are going to live in a fallen world, you are going to have to live with the implications of a fallen world. That means that you have to face the fact of natural disaster. I don't like it any more than you like it, but it is a reality that only the very foolish, the very naive, or the very stupid will pretend doesn't exist.

You Can't Be Perfect

He had struggled with temptation, and he was a Christian. People had quoted 1 Corinthians 10:13 to him. I had told him that there was no temptation which was not common to everyone and that God would provide a way out. He had prayed; he had read the Bible; he had talked to friends who promised to pray for him; he had read numerous books on temptation.

When he called me his sobs were so heavy I could hardly make out the words. "I've fallen," he said, "and now I will never be able to look at any of my Christian friends again. I don't think God will listen to my prayers anymore."

Of course, God did listen to his prayers again, and his Christian friends loved him and supported him through the crisis. He was forgiven, and now he understands God's grace. But the question he asked me after he had been restored still haunts me sometimes. "Pastor, I think I did it all right. Why did I fall?"

Secondly, sin is a part of a fallen world. Someone has said that we sin because Adam sinned and we sin as Adam sinned. Paul put it this way: "For . . . by one man's disobedience many were made sinners" (Rom. 5:19a).

There are two basic views with regard to human nature: 1) Man is basically good with an inclination toward evil, and 2) man is basically evil with an inclination toward good. The Bible takes the second of those two options. "The heart is deceitful above all things, and desperately wicked; Who can know it?" (Jer. 17:9).

You must face the fact that, because of your sin nature, you aren't perfectable. And your lack of perfectability will cause you all kinds of trouble.

There was a time in my life when I thought that if I tried hard enough and prayed long enough and studied deep enough, I would reach the point of total commitment. Then, I would be able to serve as a model to those who were less spiritual than I was. Every time I would get rid of one sin, however, the Father would show me two more. It was almost as if someone had changed the rules in the middle of the game.

A lot of years have passed, and I am wiser than I was then. The Father has taught me that He did not reveal the depth of my sin all at once because I couldn't have stood it. It would have been too devastating to my fledgling Christian life. And so He let me understand His love and His grace before He let me see the extent and the depth of my sin.

If you haven't discovered Thomas à Kempis's *Imitation of Christ*, you have missed one of the great devotional masterpieces of the Christian faith. During his more than ninety years of life, Thomas à Kempis (Thomas Hammerken) achieved a depth of meditative understanding rarely seen in the church. Often when I am spiritually dry, I will open *Imitation* and find great blessing from the words of this very wise Augustinian monk.

Thomas à Kempis wrote of our inability to understand our motivations and sin:

We cannot trust much to ourselves, because grace oftentimes is wanting to us, and understanding also. There is but little light in us, and that which we have we quickly lose by our negligence. Oftentimes too we do not perceive our own inward blindness how great it is. We often do evil, and excuse it worse. We are sometimes moved with passion, and we think it to be zeal. We reprehend small things in others, and pass over greater matters in ourselves. We quickly enough feel and weigh what we suffer at the hands of others; but we mind not what others suffer from us. He that well and rightly considereth his own works, will find little cause to judge hardly of another.

I suspect that if we could somehow live a life of perfect obedience to God, we could live a life without a lot of the hassles and hurts we must face. The problem is that we can't. We can get better; we can improve; we can, in John Wesley's words, "move on to perfection." But perfection is something we will not obtain until we get home to heaven: "It has not yet been revealed what we shall be, but we know that when He is revealed, we shall be like Him" (1 John 3:2b).

The late Art DeMoss, one of the great personal evangelists of our time, used to reply to someone who asked him how he was, "Better than I deserve." Christians need to recognize that things are bad because we are bad, and if things were as bad as we deserved, they would be a whole lot worse.

Not only does our own sin create a problem, but also the sin of others creates a problem with BRS. In Florida one of the slogans of our highway department is Drive Defensively. That's a good idea, but on the streets of Miami, it isn't good enough. No matter how much

17

you watch the other drivers, you can't watch all of them all of the time. Someday, someone is going to get you.

Sin is like that. The world is made in such a way that you suffer for others' sin. (I know. I don't like it either, but we're talking about what is and not what we wish would be.) The drunk who runs over a youngster, the parent who abuses his or her child, the expedient decisions of bad politicians, the specter of terrorism, the pollution of the city, the horror of war: on and on, we can list the sinful actions of others that deeply affect our lives. Even if we could be perfect—which we can't—we would still have problems caused by the imperfections of others.

Jesus often spoke of Christians as being *in* the world but not being *of* the world. While we are in the world, we must recognize and accept the reality and the repercussions of sin. It doesn't do any good to get mad. Sin just is.

She was the daughter of one of the finest Christian families in our church. She was a "good girl" with a sterling witness for Christ. When she called me that morning, she said it was important to see me that day. Something deep inside told me that whatever she wanted to talk to me about was not good.

"I'm pregnant," she said, holding back the tears, "and Bill says he won't marry me. He is the first man I have had sexual relations with and only with him because I was so sure that he was the one. I feel so ashamed."

Abortion was out of the question, her father said, when we went to him. The family handled the news quite well. They stood beside her, and when the baby was born, he became a much loved part of the extended family. Our church stood with

*the whole family, and when the child was baptized, there was
not a dry eye in the congregation.*

*But there were questions: How could such good parents
have this happen to their daughter? Did they do something
wrong? She was such a great witness for Christ. Where did she
go wrong?*

The Sting of Death

There is one more implication of the Fall I don't want
you to miss—the reality of death. Please note the implication of Romans 5:12: "Therefore, just as through one
man sin entered the world, and death through sin, and
thus death spread to all men, because all sinned." Paul
says in 1 Corinthians 15:56 that the "sting of death is
sin." In other words, the ultimate result of sin is death.

Have you ever had someone tell you not worry
about death, because it was as natural as birth and just a
part of life? They lied to you! Death is not natural. We
were not born to die. Disease and death are the result of
sin.

Every once in a while I will hear someone say at a
funeral as they look into a casket, "He [or she] looks so
good." I want to say, "You've got to be kidding! He's
dead!" Of course, I never say anything like that, but I
have never found death to be a very nice or pretty thing.
However, it is a reality—a fact—with which Christians
must deal.

As I was flying from Miami to Los Angeles for a
speaking engagement a couple of years ago, it became
apparent that the teenage girl in the aisle across from me
was in desperate trouble. She had been terminally ill, her
mother said, for almost two years, but her family had not

expected anything to happen this soon. The flight attendants found three doctors who worked on the young woman in a futile attempt to save her life.

When she died, the pilot landed the plane in Dallas, and all the passengers were taken from the plane. We watched as the young woman's shrouded body was carried down the side steps of the 747 to a waiting hearse.

Evidently most of the passengers in my section of the plane had been on a cruise together out of Miami. They had come on the plane in a "party" mood, laughing and joking with one another—trying, I suppose, to prolong the fun they had enjoyed on the cruise.

The death of the young woman spoiled their fun. When the passengers again boarded the plane, they were a different crowd, somber and quiet.

Because I deal often with death, I informed the flight attendant that I was a pastor and if I could help I would be glad to do anything I could. "I appreciate your offer," she said, "but we've decided to give all of the passengers free drinks. That ought to make them feel better."

If I could have preached to that group of passengers, I believe they would have become Christians. For the first time they were facing the unpleasant reality of death, and they couldn't get away from it. (One doesn't leave a 747 that's flying at thirty-four thousand feet.) I wanted to tell them about Jesus and His promise of eternal life. But the world deals with death in a far different way. They try to forget it, to ignore it, and that being impossible, they try to drink away the reality.

A Christian can't afford to do that. Biblical Christian realism requires that you look at death and disease in the face. Sickness and death are like taxes; you can't avoid them forever. Anybody who tells you anything different may have all of his or her marbles, but he or she doesn't have a shooter.

Well, that's the bad news. It doesn't seem fair, and maybe it isn't. But sin and suffering are part of the reality with which we have to deal. There's more bad news, but we *will* get to the "good" stuff. Sin and suffering are only part of the reality.

If you are a Christian you have hope. And because of this hope, things *can* get better.

2

It's Not Your Party!

*H*ave you heard the story about the doctor who called his patient and said, "Jack, I have some bad news for you, and I have some very bad news for you."

"Good heavens!" the man exclaimed. "That's horrible. Tell me the bad news first."

"The bad news is that I have looked at the results of your tests, and you have less than twenty-four hours to live."

"Man! If that's the bad news, what in the world is the *very* bad news?"

"The very bad news," replied the doctor, "is that I was supposed to call you yesterday."

In the last chapter we saw the bad news about a fallen world. Now, I have some very bad news. In this chapter I want to show you our part in a fallen world. If we get through this one, it will be rather "clear sailing" to the end.

Bad news is sometimes a matter of perspective. In a sense, all true news, even if it is bad, can be good news. In other words, when you know the truth you can act accordingly. The bad news of this chapter is like that too. Because it's true, you can live by it. What is bad news to some, might be good news to others.

I was talking to a friend who was depressed one

Christmas. Her family lived over two thousand miles away, she had no husband or children, and most of her friends were involved with their families. She had celebrated Christmas with a few close friends, but she still felt empty and sad. So she prayed.

As she prayed she began to think, *Why am I so sad? This isn't my party anyway. It's not my birthday; it's Jesus' birthday.* Christmas was a celebration for Jesus, not for her, she had decided.

The rest of the day she spent in praising the One who had been born in a manger and who had loved her enough to die for her on a cross. She visited the friends of Jesus in the hospitals and the nursing homes, and then she made some resolutions about her life, which she offered to Jesus as her gift for His birthday.

The good news in this chapter is you have been invited to a party. The bad news is that it isn't your party. If you think it is your party and you act accordingly, then the news of this chapter is going to be very bad indeed. But once you understand the One for whom the party is given, all things considered, it isn't such a bad party after all.

Understanding the Way the World Works

Remember the story of Job? He had the kind of life about which most of us can only dream. He had money, prestige, a going business, and a wonderful family. Then God allowed all of that to be taken away. In other words, Job's rope broke.

Job asked all of the questions you and I would have asked in that situation: Why me? Why would God allow all of this to happen to me? Have I been so bad that I should be punished in this way? Almost all of the book

23

of Job consists of philosophical and theological discussions dealing with Job's problems. Like many similar discussions, they resolve nothing.

Finally, God comes to Job and asks a series of questions that are nothing less than "mind blowing." (You will find those questions in Job 38–41. As God questions Job, Job begins to realize something he hadn't seen before. He realizes that the world doesn't revolve around him. He is God's servant, not the other way around. And as Job begins to understand the way the world works—as the light dawns—he finds that it wasn't what he expected.

Finally, in the last chapter of the book, we hear Job say to God,

> *"I have heard of You by the hearing of the ear,*
> *But now my eye sees You.*
> *Therefore I abhor myself,*
> *And repent in dust and ashes."*
> *Job 42:5–6*

Someone tells of a large company where the president set a goal that everyone would contribute to the United Fund. So everybody in the company gave, except one man. The other employees tried their best to convince the man to give. They appealed to his philanthropic nature; they told him about the great needs in the community; they told him how important it was to be a part of the team. He still refused to give.

The president of the company finally called the man into his office and said, "Sam, it is my desire that this company be a part of the United Fund, and it is my desire that our participation be 100 percent. There are two ways we will reach that level of giving. If you give, we will meet my goal, or if you don't give, I will fire you and we will meet my goal."

"Of course, I will give," the man responded. "It's just that nobody ever explained it that way to me before."

That's what happened to Job. When God explained the situation, Job said, "Nobody ever explained it that way to me before. I repent in dust and ashes."

If you are going to play in any sport, you need to understand the rules. If you're going to work successfully in any enterprise, you need to understand the way that enterprise works.

When I was in school, I was never a very good student until I understood the system. After that I wasn't a better student, but I played the game better and received outstanding grades. The world is sort of like that. You have to understand how the world works to live appropriately.

God's Plan, Not Ours

St. Teresa of Avila, the Spanish contemplative of the sixteenth century, had a delightful sense of humor. She would say, "Lord, You would have more friends if You treated the ones You had better." I love that comment, but the presupposition may not be true; that is, God's goal in the world may not be to make friends.

Our fallen nature is egocentric. That's another way of saying that most of us in our heart of hearts believe that the world revolves around us. The titles of most of the books we read (including this one) indicate that the books will in some way make our lives better. We read books on how to have more power in our prayer life, how to become thin and beautiful, how to make our marriages sparkle, and how to have a faith that works. Now there is, of course, nothing wrong with those books or the promises they make. But we may have missed the point.

The Bible teaches that the world was not created for us; it was created by and for God: "'To whom then will you liken Me, / Or to whom shall I be equal?' says the Holy One" (Isa. 40:25). The world was created by God so that His attributes might be seen: "Since the creation of the world His invisible attributes are clearly seen, being understood by the things that are made, even His eternal power and Godhead" (Rom. 1:20). The reason for creation is that God might be glorified: "The heavens declare the glory of God; / And the firmament shows His handiwork" (Ps. 19:1). When we look at the creation of God, our response should be the response of the living creatures in Revelation: "You are worthy, O Lord, to receive glory and honor and power; for You created all things, and by Your will they exist and were created" (Rev. 4:11).

God has created the world for His reasons and not for ours. That is the very bad news.

I attended a worship service one Sunday with an architect friend of mine. The church building had a very modern design. As we sat together before the service began, he leaned over to me and said, "Pastor, do you know what they say about the building of this church?" I shook my head no. "They say that when they were building it, there was a heavy rain, and the plans got wet and wrinkled. They built it anyway."

That church looked weird to me. But, you see, I

wasn't the architect. I suspect that the building turned out exactly the way he planned it.

The world is sort of like that church building. If the world doesn't make us happy it's good to remember that the world wasn't created to make us happy. If things are not to our liking, it's good to remember that things were not created to be to our liking. If we think that things are mixed up, we may simply not understand the Architect's plans.

Gaining Perspective on the Rope

We must understand early in our discussion of Broken Rope Syndrome that breaking ropes, as horrible as they are, may be seen from another perspective. We feel, when the rope breaks and the tragedy follows, that something is out of control. But that may not be the case. Breaking ropes are not necessarily the major concern of God. He may have other priorities.

A number of years ago there was a popular song which asked the question, "What's it all about, Alfie?" That really is our question when the rope breaks, isn't it? A woman who had been through a time of great loss in her family once told me, "Pastor, I could stand all of this if I just knew there was a reason for it." The rope's breaking is not the central problem we face. Our real problem is the seeming meaninglessness of the breaking ropes. When the rope breaks and there seems to be no reason, no meaning behind the breaking rope, the hurt we experience is compounded.

You do have a choice in how you view the world after your rope has broken, you know. You have at least three ways to look at the world where your rope has broken.

This Isn't Really Happening

You can choose to believe that the world is a wonderful playground created by a benevolent Creator for your enjoyment and pleasure. With this belief, you will see your broken rope as a temporary aberration in the norm, or you will pretend that the broken rope really isn't broken.

In the book of Job, one of Job's false friends, Eliphaz, told Job his present experiences were only temporary; they would soon pass over. "He [God] shall deliver you in six troubles, / Yes, in seven no evil shall touch you" (Job 5:19).

Now, there is nothing wrong with Eliphaz's advice to Job. In fact, in many situations it would be the proper thing to say. The problem with applying it to Job is that it simply wasn't true. Having read the first two chapters of Job, we know the truth.

Job's reply to Eliphaz cuts through what, in this case, was simply the wrong thing to say to a hurting man:

> *"Teach me, and I will hold my tongue;*
> *Cause me to understand wherein I have erred.*
> *How forceful are right words!*
> *But what does your arguing prove?*
> *Do you intend to reprove my words,*
> *And the speeches of a desperate one, which are as wind?*
> *Yes, you overwhelm the fatherless,*
> *And you undermine your friend.*
> *Now therefore, be pleased to look at me;*
> *For I would never lie to your face."*
>
> *Job 6:24–28*

When I watch a person who is facing tragedy and pretending that the tragedy doesn't exist, I am reminded of the story of the three men who found themselves in hell. One was a Presbyterian, another was a Baptist, and the third was a member of one of the mind-science religions.

The Presbyterian said, "I wish I had paid attention to my pastor. He was a Bible teacher, and if I had only listened then, I wouldn't be here."

"My pastor," said the Baptist, "always was clear about the way to go to heaven. I just didn't believe him. If I had believed him, I wouldn't be here now."

But the mind-science religionist sat over in the corner with his head in his hands, repeating over and over, "It's not hot and I'm not here. It's not hot and I'm not here. It's not hot and I'm not here. . . ."

Positive thinking can be an effective way to make your life better, but positive thinking simply doesn't work when the rope has broken. You can pretend that the rope is still holding you, but you can't will it back together. All of the wishing in the world is not going to make the ground come up more slowly when you're falling toward it. Pretending that you live in a world where failures and tragedies don't happen—or if they do they are only temporary—is going to require a lot of pretending.

An old Chinese story tells of a thief who stole a bell. As he was rushing away from the place where he had stolen the bell, he found that he couldn't keep the bell from ringing. In his panic and his fear of being discovered, he came upon a way to feel safe. He covered his ears so he couldn't hear the bell.

The real world is no place to cover your ears or eyes. Playing pretend may be O.K. for children but not for the man or woman of God. Yet that is exactly what a lot of Christians do. Anyone who has ever faced a tragedy straight-on has heard and winced at some of the clichés people use when trying to give comfort. People will say, "I know it's bad now, but you'll be better for it." "Sometimes God loves us so much that He allows us to suffer." "It's always darkest before the dawn." "Great good will come out of this."

Now much of that may be true, but it is desperately important that a Christian not hide behind clichés and pious platitudes.

Death is, perhaps, the thing we fear most. Too many Christians glibly talk about how they have no fear of death, and more often than not, I don't believe them. In fact, most people who say they have no fear of death are simply denying a reality they'll eventually have to face. The statistic is always one out of one.

Fear of death is normal, and the best way to deal with the fear is to face it head-on. The English proverb about dealing with fear is right: Fear knocked at the door. Faith answered. No one was there.

Sometimes you can't deal with the fear of death all at once. (I'm talking about facing the fact that *you* are going to die, to cease to exist in your present form, to be buried in a casket.) Sometimes you have to face that reality a little at a time, like going swimming in a cold stream. You start with your big toe and work up slowly. If a Christian deals with the fear of death by facing it even for short periods and building up slowly, he or she will eventually be able to look the grim reaper straight in the face without trembling. Because death is not a little thing, anyone who explains it away with platitudes is in for a horrible surprise. How much better to face the fear of death as a normal part of living. We can deal with it by first facing the reality that it will happen and *then* claiming the promises of God related to it. The problem happens when Christians claim the promises without facing the reality. They are, then, not dealing with the problem of the fear but rather denying that the problem exists.

Examples can be multiplied over and over again of Christians' denying the reality not only of death, specifically, but also of broken ropes, generally. Parents, even when confronted with incontrovertible evidence, will deny that their son or daughter is on drugs or into any other trouble. For most Christians, self-analysis rarely yields much real knowledge of their sin. We pretend that by quoting Romans 8:28 we won't experience any real hurt or pain. We deny our doubts thereby making our faith a fantasy. We deny the pain of growth thereby becoming stunted. We deny the harshness of God thereby becoming worshipers of idols.

For a while our proclaiming that God has created the world for our enjoyment and pleasure may work. But that choice is essentially a game of self-delusion. Someone told of a man who had fallen out of a window on the twentieth floor of a twenty-story building. As he passed the floors below, he was heard mumbling to himself, "I'm O.K. so far. I'm O.K. so far. I'm O.K. so far."

All Is Vanity

You can adopt a second view of the world where your rope has broken. You can choose to believe that the world is essentially meaningless. In other words, you can say with Macbeth, "Life's but a walking shadow, a

31

poor player, / And then is heard no more; it is a tale Told by an idiot, full of sound and fury, / Signifying nothing."

If you're looking for a world without meaning, you can find plenty of evidence. The Preacher, the author of Ecclesiastes, wrote:

> *What profit has a man from all his labor*
> *In which he toils under the sun?*
> *One generation passes away, and another generation comes;*
> *But the earth abides forever. . . .*
> . . . .
> *I have seen all the works that are done under the sun; and*
> *indeed, all is vanity and grasping for the wind.*
> *Eccles. 1:3–4,14*

The Preacher was simply saying, "Men must work, and women must weep, and the sooner it's over, the sooner to sleep." Or, as I read on a bumper sticker the other day: "Life is hard, and then you die."

Meaninglessness is a choice we make. When Camus said that the only question with which modern man must deal is the question of suicide, he understood perfectly the dilemma we face. What is our purpose for living? Do we have any? Only the very silly believe that the world is a playground filled with good things for God's children. There is simply too much hurt and loneliness and death and evil. If we are not so silly as to accept that kind of option, without God, our only other option is meaninglessness.

If you've chosen that option and the rope breaks, you can create meaning in the breaking rope as long as you realize that the meaning you've created is not ultimate. Whether you want to devote your life to stepping on Dixie Cups or to helping the poor, it doesn't matter—you can invest meaning into your tasks. But don't ever fool yourself into believing that the broken rope has meaning beyond what you've assigned. Ultimately, all is vanity.

A prominent sociologist has said that you can tell a lot about a society by observing the way the people in that society dance. He commented, after visiting a disco, that Americans dance the way people on the *Titanic* would dance—the dance of meaninglessness and death. I can imagine the janitor of a disco. After all the lights are dimmed, the blaring speakers are turned off, the band has gone home, and the dance floor is empty, he sweeps up the debris left by the dancers. He pauses to rest, leans on his broom, and asks himself, "What was all that about?" He thinks for a moment and replies to his own question: "It was about nothing—nothing at all."

That, of course, is an option for those who are trying to understand what the world is all about. If there is no God, there is no meaning; and if there is no meaning, there is no value to your life with or without broken ropes. And if there is no value, you might as well be a turnip. As long as you remember that, you can keep on until you die, and, who knows? You might have a little fun on the way.

God Is Everything

The final option if you're asking questions about the meaning of breaking ropes poses a Creator who, for His own reasons, created the world. That is the biblical option, and while it isn't altogether great news, it, at least, brings genuine meaning into the equation.

One of the reasons I believe in the Christian faith is

because no one would make up the stuff we believe. I have, in my day, been a reasonably good liar, and I know (as does every proficient liar) that a lie, in order to be believed, must not stray too far from the reality of the one who is presented with the lie.

When one considers the Christian faith, one must face the fact that it is either true or one whopper of a lie. God entering time and space? In a manger, no less? Walking on water, bringing sight to the blind, raising the dead? Dying for sin on a cross? Teaching about love in the midst of a world of hatred? A dead man getting out of a grave and talking about death? Ascending into heaven in a cloud? Coming again?

You've got to be kidding!

And yet that is exactly what Christians believe! Because it is so unbelievable, so wild, so gigantic there is no way we would believe it unless it's true.

If you understand the rules of a game, you may not like the rules but you'll play a lot better. Most people, however, seem to be playing a football game with baseball rules; that is, they are living in a world with a whole set of presuppositions (I'm supposed to be happy; the world centers around me; I'm more important than anything else) which simply aren't true.

The Bible teaches that God created the world that He might be glorified. Once you understand that, you have the key to living and to dying. In the early days of this country, Puritan pastors took an extensive examination before they were ordained, covering their understanding of doctrine. One of the questions examiners often asked was, Would you be willing to be damned for the glory of God? (When one young man, who had been through a terribly grueling examination, was asked that question, he wiped the perspiration off his forehead and thought for a moment. "No," he said, "I don't think I would. However if God in His wisdom and sovereignty should decide to damn you, I wouldn't object.")

I used to think that question was irrelevant, but the older I get the more I realize that it is the central question. Would I be willing to be damned for the glory of God? I don't know. I do know, however, that the closer I can come to saying yes to that question, the closer I come to understanding what my life and the world is all about.

I think it was Toscanini who, after conducting a Beethoven symphony, said to musicians in his orchestra, "I am nothing. You are nothing. Beethoven is everything!" Just so, when you come to the place in your life where you can say, "I am nothing. God is everything," then, and only then, are you equipped to deal with the meaning behind breaking ropes.

"Our God Reigns!"

In the next chapters we will, of course, talk a lot more about this subject, and the news will get better and better as we go along. However, before you can understand the good news—indeed, before the good news can even be good—you have to understand the bad news: We live in a fallen world, and everything about it was created that God might be glorified. If you understand that one fact, breaking ropes will still hurt, but you will find the meaning in them. And if you can find the meaning, you will be able to deal with the hurt.

In March of 1984 one of the great men of God in our time, David Watson, died. Thousands of Christians (myself included) who had been blessed by his preaching and writing were devastated. Watson was only in his forties, and it seemed that he died too soon. Some would say that Watson's life was wasted. He had been pastor of a church in York and later became an evangelist, who was especially effective with young people. Why in the world would God allow someone with his gifts to die?

One of the things David Watson was known for was the way he would sometimes ask the congregations before whom he preached to stand and shout, "Our God Reigns!" I am told that the experience of shouting that truth moved many to a closer understanding of God's world and their part in it.

The week after Watson died, John Collins, an Anglican priest, was serving Holy Communion in his church. Collins was an older man, with a long life of service in the name of Christ; however, one of his greatest acts of service was to introduce David Watson to Christ. I don't know, but I suspect that as Collins went through the ancient liturgy of Communion, he must have had questions mixed with hurt over Watson's death. With much sadness he spoke of his friend David, and how he would miss him. Yet in spite of his sadness, he said he expected to see Watson again at the great Marriage Supper of the Lamb.

And then Collins did something strange for an Anglican priest. He asked the congregation (some two thousand people) to stand and to shout three times, "Our God Reigns!" Those who were there said it was one of the most moving experiences of their lives: this great throng of people, shouting in unison, "Our God Reigns! Our God Reigns! Our God Reigns!" The crowd then broke out in spontaneous applause that lasted so long, that John Collins had to finally stop it. When he did, people all over the church were weeping. God's

Spirit had come and God's people understood, perhaps not cognitively but with their hearts, what life is all about.

Life is about the King. It is not about His servants, or His lands, or His subjects. It is *only* about the King. In the midst of breaking ropes, our God reigns.

If you understand that—I mean, really understand that—and you belong to Him, you can face almost anything.

3

The Very, Very Good News

*I*f you're still with me, you now have two important facts to remember when your rope breaks. First, we live in a fallen world where broken ropes are a fact of life. Second, the world is not created for our purposes, but for God's purposes. If you have come this far, you have some questions: If this is God's world, what is God like? Do we live in a world where God takes perverted delight in breaking our ropes? Is God's nature, thus His creation, benevolent or malevolent? Are our broken ropes related to God's purposes, or do we just have to accept misery as ordained by a sovereign God, without any reference to us or to our needs?

God Loves You a Lot

Paul said,

What shall we say then? Is there unrighteousness with God? Certainly not! For He says to Moses, "I will have mercy on whomever I will have mercy, and I will have compassion on whomever I will have compassion." So then it is not of him who wills, nor of him who runs, but of God who shows mercy.
Rom. 9:14–16

I spend a lot of time talking to people who are, they think, having intellectual problems with the Christian faith. Recently, a young woman told me that she would like to believe in Christ, but she couldn't because her mind kept getting in the way. "I think that the Bible is a nice idea," she said, "but one has to give up thinking to believe it."

She found, however, that the Christian world view was the only world view which made any intellectual sense. I gave her a number of books to read and we set a time to meet again.

When she came back to my study, her whole demeanor had changed. "I'm reading the books you gave me," she said, "and I am finding a whole new world I never knew existed." Then she said rather sheepishly, "I've also been reading the Bible." I asked her what she had discovered there.

"Well, I started in Genesis and have read to the middle of Exodus. And," she continued, "I am finding out a lot about God. The problem is that I don't like the God I'm finding very much."

I asked my friend if she knew what idolatry was. She said she didn't, so I explained that creating and worshiping a god who measures up to our own standards is idolatry.

"You know," I said, "if you kept searching until you found a god you liked, he wouldn't be God."

"I see what you mean," she said. "The issue is the existence of God. If there really is a God, then I must come to Him on His terms and not mine."

"Bingo!" I replied with my customary dignity and perception.

If God loves you, it isn't because He has to love you. If He is going to help you with your broken ropes it isn't because He has to help you with them. And if He's going to make your breaking rope fit into a plan that is ultimately good, it isn't because He has to make it fit.

Here, then, is the good news for the believer: God does love you and He loves you a whole lot.

"Behold what manner of love the Father has bestowed on us, that we should be called children of God!" (1 John 3:1). "In this is love, not that we loved God, but that He loved us and sent His Son to be the propitiation for our sins" (1 John 4:10).

Now , if your rope has broken, how do you reconcile that with the fact that God loves you? When told that the reason he suffered so much was that God loved him, a friend of mine replied, "Well, that's nice, I suppose. But I wish He loved me a little less." I suspect you feel that way at times: If God loves me, He has a strange way of showing it.

Well, maybe not so strange. Let's talk about it.

What Does His Love Mean?

What I'm going to say may not be new to many of you, but it is very important. The Greeks had a number of words which are translated into the English word *love*. They had a word for brotherly love and erotic love and love of things. But the New Testament word used more often than any other for *love* was *agape*. Interestingly, the word *agape* wasn't used much by the Greeks until Christians started using it. The Greeks spoke of a love for the deserving, a love that sought to possess.

The love of the New Testament is quite different. Agape means to love the unlovely, to be benevolent and filled with good will, no matter what the response of the loved one. Paul said, "But God demonstrates His own love *(agape)* for us, in that while we were still sinners,

Christ died for us" (Rom. 5:8). So, when the Bible says that you are loved, there are some wonderful implications that apply directly to your broken rope.

Your Broken Rope Has Purpose

First, because God loves you and values you, your broken rope has purpose. Did you know that in the early days of plastic surgery, some people believed that the results wouldn't be good if an anesthetic was used? In those days, if you wanted to change what God had given you, you had to endure a lot of pain.

God is fulfilling His purpose in you, in others, and in the world. You can't get from here to there without hurt. Just as the early beliefs about plastic surgery entailed pain for gain, the only way to make significant progress is to endure some significant suffering and pain. If you want to have muscles, you have to work at it, and as you work at it, you'll discover a high degree of soreness. If you want to play a musical instrument, you have to go through hours of sour notes and grueling practice. If you want to get a good education, you have to burn the midnight oil and suffer from bloodshot eyes and sleepless nights.

I bought an exercise machine a couple of years ago. The advertisement said that if I exercised only ten minutes a day, I would have a flat stomach and a muscular shape. That wasn't true. You can't get that kind of figure in ten minutes a day. I tried—I really tried. An investment of ten minutes in almost anything will bring a very small yield. Flat stomachs and muscular shapes don't come easy. Nothing does.

Now, take all the above, and apply it to your broken rope. Your tragedy and hurt is fulfilling a just, right, and proper purpose. What is that purpose? To be perfectly honest with you, I don't know.

Sometimes we are missing the one thing we would like to know—what is God accomplishing through our suffering? Oh, there are indications from Scripture, and sometimes God allows us to see what is being accomplished. But a lot of times we simply are not allowed to know what God is doing. What we do know is that God, because He loves us, is doing what is necessary.

I'm told that there is one species of birds of which the mother bird does everything she can to get her growing babies out of the nest. When she is ready for them to go and she knows that they can fly, she begins to push them out of the nest. On occasion, when a particularly recalcitrant bird refuses to leave the nest, the mother does what a lot of human mothers ought to do when their children refuse to grow up. She actually begins to take the nest away. Piece by piece she picks at the nest until it is completely dismantled. I can imagine a conversation going on between the child and the mother.

"Mother!" the small bird shouts. "What are you doing?"

"I'm taking your nest away," she replies.

"Why are you doing that?"

"I put it up. I can take it down."

"But don't you love me?"

"Of course, I love you. But my love requires that you fly, and you can't fly sitting around in that nest all the time. So, I'm taking it away."

The small bird suddenly finds itself sitting on thin air and begins to flap its wings. As it flies upward, surprised at its ability, it calls back over its shoulder, "Hey, Mom. Look at me. I'm flying! I'm flying!"

"Of course, you're flying," the mother says. "That's what the disappearing nest is all about."

Sometimes we're allowed to see the reason for our pain. But there are other times when we simply have to trust that God loves us and that He knows what He's doing. Do you remember the time Jesus washed the disciples' feet? As Jesus was going around the table, stopping at the place of each disciple, Peter became irritated. He simply couldn't understand why the Son of God should be washing anybody's feet. It ought to be the other way around, he thought. And then Jesus said, "What I am doing you do not understand now, but you will know after this" (John 13:7).

Jesus was telling Peter to trust Him. He was saying, "I'm doing right, and you'll understand. But for now just trust me." God says that to us a lot. Your broken rope has a purpose. That purpose may be to bring you to a place of greater love and balance. Sometimes that purpose has to do with others. In that case, we can identify with Christ because He vicariously suffered for us. The purpose may have nothing to do with you or anybody you know, and when you get to heaven you'll find out that your suffering was a part of a great, ultimately good plan, which you could not have understood even if God had explained it to you at the time.

I suspect that God says to those who have a broken rope (if we listen), "Child, I know it hurts. I know your fear and your emptiness. If there was a way your finite mind could understand, I would explain it to you. I want you to remember that if there was any other way, I would have chosen it. But there isn't, so hang tough and someday you will understand."

"But Steve," you are saying, "that takes a lot of

faith." Of course it does. "We walk by faith, not by sight" (2 Cor. 5:7). His gift to you is faith. You simply have to ask Him for it. We'll have a lot more to say about this in a later chapter, but for now, remember that if God loves you, nothing is happening to you without a significant, important, and loving purpose.

You *Will* Make It Through

Because God loves and values you, your broken rope will not ultimately destroy you. Job was afraid that the pain he was suffering would destroy him: "Cease! Leave me alone, that I may take a little comfort, / Before I go to the place from which I shall not return" (Job 10:20–21).

Job's fears of total destruction were groundless. If he had known that God loved and valued him, he would perhaps have made a different speech. And then again, maybe he wouldn't have. When your rope is broken, it's hard to be rational and to draw legitimate conclusions from the facts. At any rate, although Job's friends said some insensitive things, on occasion they spoke the truth. Let me give you a portion of an absolutely true speech from his friend Bildad. Bildad assures Job that Job won't be destroyed by his suffering.

> *"Behold, this is the joy of His way,*
> *And out of the earth others will grow.*
> *Behold, God will not cast away the blameless,*
> *Nor will He uphold the evildoers.*
> *He will yet fill your mouth with laughing,*
> *And your lips with rejoicing.*
> *Those who hate you will be clothed with shame,*
> *And the dwelling place of the wicked will come to nothing."*
> *Job 8:19–22*

I have a friend who is going through a mid-life crisis, and he is experiencing the struggles that come along about the age of forty. "Steve," he said the other day, "mid-life crisis isn't so bad because you know that you go from mid-life to maturity. It's the old age crisis that will get me, because death follows old age." That's the great fear we have when our rope breaks—that death will follow.

Let me give you a working principle: You can stand any tough times if you know they are only temporary. If you know that the suffering will end, you can get through it. God promises that, though it may hurt now, there will come an end, and you will not ultimately be destroyed. His love assures that "bottom-line" fact.

Both of our daughters have made good grades in school. However, when Robin, one of our daughters, was taking an advanced English class in high school, she came to me after a couple of sessions and said, "Dad, I can't take that course. Everyone in the course is ahead of me, and half the time I don't know what's going on. I want to take a regular English class."

Her request seemed reasonable to me, so I went with her to the high school to change the course from advanced English to the regular English course. The advisor said that, of course, Robin could change, but she would need the approval of the head of the English department.

And so Robin and I made our way to the office of the head of the English department, Jenny Krugman, who is a delight. She told me that if I wanted Robin to change, she would approve it, but she asked me if it would be O.K. if she talked to Robin first. I nodded my approval, and she turned to Robin. "Robin, almost everyone who takes this advanced English course is frightened at the beginning. If we didn't think you could do it, we would never have assigned you to the course. It will be hard, but you can do the work."

Robin wasn't buying a word of it until Jenny said, "Robin, I am going to make you a deal. I promise that, no matter how bad your work is, you will get at least a B in this course. If I promise you that, will you take the course?"

Now, Robin isn't dumb. She knows a good deal when she sees one, and she accepted it. Robin ended up making straight A's in the course for the next two years and majored in English at college. Later Jenny explained her theory to me. "I knew your daughter could do the work," she said, "but she didn't know it. So I took the threat of failure away by promising her a good grade no matter what. I couldn't have done that with a lot of students, but I knew I was safe with Robin."

You see, Robin was afraid of failure. As soon as she knew she wasn't going to fail the course, she was free to study hard. The work wasn't easy for her, but advanced English was her most productive course that year.

God treats us like Jenny Krugman treated Robin. In Christ, He has taken away the threat of ultimate destruction. He has said, "I promise you that you will come out of this fine." Once we know that, we can deal with a broken rope.

You Are Not Alone

Because God loves you and values you, you do not have to bear the pain of your broken rope alone. Jesus· said:

"I will pray the Father, and He will give you another Helper, that He may abide with you forever, even the Spirit of truth,

whom the world cannot receive, because it neither sees Him nor knows Him; but you know Him, for He dwells with you and will be in you. I will not leave you orphans; I will come to you."
John 14:16–18

In an interview with William Buckley, Malcolm Muggeridge was discussing the concept of the Cross. Buckley talked about people he had known who had suffered and yet were serene. Muggeridge responded:

In every time, and in every age, this [the spiritual benefits of suffering] is demonstrated to us, and I think in our time it's been marvelously demonstrated by Solzhenitsyn and the other heroic people from the Soviet labour camps, all of whom say the same thing—the ones that have achieved spiritual perception through it—that there they learned this point, that it's through the affliction that you can see reality and that, therefore, as Solzhenistsyn himself says in his Gulag book, "Thank you, prison camp, for bringing this illumination into my life which otherwise I would have lost."[1]

Now, you must be very careful here. This whole concept can easily become a cliché offered to people whose ropes have broken. And I suspect that anyone who has not suffered, or who is not suffering right now, doesn't have the right to talk glibly about the presence of God in the midst of suffering. Nevertheless, there are some things about God you cannot learn until the rope has broken.

Corrie ten Boom was speaking one time to some people who were facing death in the midst of persecution, and she became acutely aware that some of the people would die for Christ. Knowing they were afraid, she told them that when she was a little girl she would often go to the train station with her father, where he would put her on the train to visit relatives. Her father never gave her the money for the ticket until after she got on the train. She told those fearful people that God was like that. When it came time for them to suffer and even to die, their heavenly Father would give them the money for the ticket. The money for the ticket would be the presence of the Comforter, God's Spirit, Who, when our ropes are broken, comforts and sustains us.

A number of years ago my friend, John DeBrine, was going to have some major surgery. John believes strongly in the doctrine of Dying Grace: that God gives a special calming grace when it is the believer's time to die. Late the night before his surgery, I went to visit John at New England Baptist Hospital. I'll never forget that evening. I sat beside his bed and asked him if he was afraid.

"Of course, I'm afraid," he said. Then laughing, he added, "But I'll tell you something else. If I weren't afraid, I would be really afraid!"

I love Ron Dunn's comment: "People are always saying, 'Jesus is all I need.' You will never know Jesus is all you need until Jesus is all you've got. And when Jesus is all you've got, then and only then, will you know that Jesus is all you need." Jesus is present when your rope breaks. Sometimes you can know Him then in ways far deeper than when the pastures are green and the water is still.

As a pastor I see a lot of suffering. I am often standing around when ropes break. Time after time I have seen Jesus come when people are hurting, and that is a great fact Christians need to remember.

A little over a year ago my brother Ron died suddenly of a coronary. In his forties, he was a popular public servant, a superb district attorney, a good father, and my closest friend. I never even got a chance to say good-bye.

Three or four weeks after his death, while visiting my mother, I went to the cemetery in the mountains where we had buried Ron. It was a cold, rainy, late winter afternoon—the kind of weather that chills your bones.

When I got to the cemetery I couldn't find the place where Ron was buried. A stone had not yet been placed on his grave, and a number of others had been buried in the same general area.

As I stood in the cold and wind and rain, I began to sob. "God, this has been the worst month of my life, and now I can't even find my brother's grave."

Jesus doesn't visit cemeteries often, but He did that day. I knew there was a presence, the presence of the One I had almost forgotten in all my grief and the grief of my family. Jesus came and said, "Why are you seeking the living among the dead?" Those words comforted me, and I haven't been back to the cemetery since. I don't need to go back. The One who loved Ron and knew him came to me in my moment of grief. He promised never to leave, and that has made all the difference in the world.

It's been a difficult year since Ron died. Among other things, my wife's father died, and our grief doubled. But never once were we left alone. In the midst of our tragedy and suffering, we found Jesus.

In the midst of *your* tragedy and suffering, you will find Jesus.

You Are Becoming like Christ

Because God loves you and values you, God will use your broken rope to allow you to think His thoughts

49

after Him, to become like Him and reflect His character. Paul wrote, "We are hard pressed on every side, yet not crushed; we are perplexed, but not in despair; persecuted, but not forsaken; struck down, but not destroyed—always carrying about in the body the dying of the Lord Jesus, that the life of Jesus may be manifested in our body. For we who live are always delivered to death for Jesus' sake, that the life of Jesus also may be manifested in our mortal flesh" (2 Cor. 4:8–11). Peter said, "Beloved, do not think it strange concerning the fiery trial which is to try you, as though some strange thing happened to you; but rejoice to the extent that you partake of Christ's sufferings" (1 Peter 4:12–13a).

Jesus spoke of the believer's identifying with Him in suffering: "If the world hates you, you know that it hated Me before it hated you. If you were of the world, the world would love its own. Yet because you are not of the world, but I chose you out of the world, therefore the world hates you. Remember the word that I said to you, 'A servant is not greater than his master.' If they persecuted Me, they will also persecute you" (John 15:18–20).

The point is this: If you have never suffered, it is hard to see things from the perspective of those who suffer. And it is particularly hard to see things from Christ's perspective.

I have a serious problem with "prosperity theology," which claims that God will always heal every hurt, disease, and infirmity in this life. Many people think that it is God's will for all Christians to be prosperous and happy. God does not delight in our suffering, and sometimes He heals in miraculous ways. However, taking that truth and universalizing it is not faith—it is presumption.

When our first daughter was born, I fainted, and

when our second daughter was born, I almost killed all three of us on the way to the hospital. When I got to the hospital, the doctor told me that the baby wouldn't be coming for a long time and I should go home. (Later I found out that he took one look at me and decided I had no business being around during childbirth.) When my wife, Anna, went through pain, I went through pain. When she was sick in the early months of pregnancy, I was sick.

Now when mothers talk about the pain of childbirth, they can't say to me, "Steve, only a mother can understand!" I can understand because I experienced the trauma of childbirth right along with Anna.

Let me tell you something important. If you have never suffered, you don't have the right to offer advice to or pass judgment on those who have. You simply don't have the data with which to understand their experience. Jesus bore intense pain, and only when I bear intense pain can I even begin to understand something of His thoughts and His love.

A friend of mine went through a horrible bout with cancer. Although he is now in remission, he suffered greatly at the time. I visited him often and knew he was in agony. Then one day I came to his room in the hospital and he had changed radically. He was still suffering, but there was a radiance about him I had not seen before. When I asked him what had happened, he said, "Pastor, I was praying last night and telling Christ that I couldn't stand it much more. He spoke to me and said, 'I know how you feel. I've been there too.' Then I realized that in my suffering I could identify with Christ in a way I had never known before. Jesus and I are brothers in suffering, and now I can see some things from His perspective."

51

When your rope breaks it is never pleasant, but at that point you can begin to understand in a deeper way the sacrifice and suffering of Christ. Don't underestimate that gift. It is the gift Paul wrote about when he said, "But indeed I also count all things loss for the excellence of the knowledge of Christ Jesus my Lord, for whom I have suffered the loss of all things, and count them as rubbish, that I may gain Christ. . . that I may know Him and the power of His resurrection, and the fellowship of His sufferings" (Phil. 3:8, 10).

Your Broken Rope Is Redemptive

Because God loves and values you, your broken rope can be redemptive. Paul said a strange thing in the book of Colossians: "I now rejoice in my sufferings for you, and fill up in my flesh what is lacking in the afflictions of Christ, for the sake His body, which is the church" (Col. 1:24). Obviously, Paul is not saying that the death of Christ needs anything else added to it. Christ's death is sufficient for the sins of the world. The Bible teaches clearly that salvation is by faith in Christ and His death alone. But the question remains, How could Paul fill what was lacking in the afflictions of Christ?

One scholar, F. F. Bruce, suggested that the key to the verse is found in the idea of the "Suffering Servant" in the book of Isaiah. In Isaiah there is a switching back and forth between the portrayal of the "Suffering Servant" as an individual, the Messiah, and as the people of God, the chosen nation of Israel. In Colossians Paul spoke about the suffering of the Body of Christ as Christ's continuing redemptive action through believers to the world.

This idea of redemptive suffering was evident in

God's message to Ananias about Paul. After Paul was blinded by his encounter with Christ on the road to Damascus, Christ directed him to the home of Ananias. Ananias was not too happy about receiving Paul, because of Paul's reputation for persecuting Christians. Then Ananias received this message from the Lord: "Go, for he [Paul] is a chosen vessel of Mine to bear My name before Gentiles, kings, and the children of Israel. For I will show him how many things he must suffer for My name's sake" (Acts 9:15–16).

Paul's willingness to suffer opened the way of salvation for the Gentiles. Paul described some of that suffering in a letter he wrote to the church at Corinth:

> *Are they ministers of Christ?—I speak as a fool—I am more: in labors more abundant, in stripes above measure, in prisons more frequently, in deaths often. From the Jews five times I received forty stripes minus one. Three times I was beaten with rods; once I was stoned; three times I was shipwrecked; a night and a day I have been in the deep; in journeys often, in perils of waters, in perils of robbers, in perils of my own countrymen, in perils of the Gentiles, in perils in the city, in perils in the wilderness, in perils in the sea, in perils among false brethren; in weariness and toil, in sleeplessness often, in hunger and thirst, in fastings often, in cold and nakedness—besides the other things, what comes upon me daily: my deep concern for all the churches.*
>
> *2 Cor. 11:23–28*

When your rope breaks, you can use it in a redemptive way. Sometimes we choose to allow the rope to break because of our love for others. Paul is a good example of that, and there are many more: the Christian who refuses to demand his or her rights because there are others who are needy; the pastor who, even though he is hurt deeply, refuses to defend himself against unfair criticism from some of his church members who are not spiritually mature; the woman who does not marry a man she loves because he is not a Christian; the businessman who decides not to bring a law suit against someone who has wronged him because he knows the suit will hurt others who are innocent. The list could be multiplied over and over again.

And then there is the witness we give when our rope breaks. That kind of suffering is redemptive too. Pat Arnold is the pastor of missions in the congregation I serve. He has a long record of service to Christ as a missionary on the field, as a mission executive of World-team, and finally, as the director of that organization. Pat was one of the last missionaries to leave Cuba when Castro came to power. In fact, he stayed longer than he should have.

He told me one time that he was absolutely devastated when he left. He had built his whole life on his work for Christ in Cuba, and when he came back to the States, he left everything that was important to him in his ministry. He remembered staying in a cold, gray Y.M.C.A. room in Miami the night he returned and feeling depressed and empty. It took him nearly two years to get back on track after leaving the people he loved so much.

I asked Pat what helped him during that time, and he, very quickly, referred to Isobel Kuhn's book *Green Leaf in Drought Time*, a book about other missionaries who were forced to leave China. In the foreword to that book, J. Oswald Sanders wrote, "God does not waste suffering, nor does He discipline out of caprice. If he plows, it is because He purposes a crop. This book shares with us the secret of that purposing and lets us see something of the crop."[2]

As Pat read that book, he received new hope and courage. Reading about others who had gone through a similar experience encouraged him to keep on serving the cause of Christ.

The suffering (BRS) of missionaries who were forced out of China was redemptive for Pat. It can happen over and over again. I have visited Christians who were dying in order to minister *to* them, and have been ministered to *by* them because of the grace with which they dealt with their suffering.

I don't like the idea of death. (I'm not afraid of death, just the process of getting there.) However, I'm praying that when my time comes to die, God will give me the grace I need. I want all of my Christian friends to invite their non-Christian friends to my deathbed, and I want the Christians to say, "Come and see how a Christian dies." If that happens, then my broken rope will be redemptive.

Suffering can also be redemptive to the one who suffers. Suffering purifies us. In other words, maturing in Christ is a process of being crucified with Christ. It means allowing our egos to die so when it comes our time to die physically, we will already understand the nature of death. Paul wrote, "I have been crucified with Christ; it is no longer I who live, but Christ lives in me; and the life which I now live in the flesh I live by faith in the Son of God, who loved me and gave Himself for me" (Gal. 2:20).

Have you noticed that much of our Christian life is ego-oriented? Because I'm a preacher, I'm often "up front" teaching the Bible at conferences and conventions.

If I don't get enough compliments on what I've done, I can get depressed. Sometimes, I fear, I am in danger of being a crowd-pleaser.

Our public prayers and testimonies often are not speaking of and glorifying God but are speaking to a crowd and glorifying self. One of the great dangers of the electronic church (of which I am a part) is that it glorifies ego and promotes testimonies pleasing to the audience rather than to the God who reigns. Much of our hymnody is geared toward a selfish and ego-satisfying type of lyric, which makes man the center of the music. Many times offices in the church are sought because of their prestige.

Living the Christian life today requires that we do a lot of dying before we die physically. There is a lot of ego that needs God's refining fire. Paul wrote:

> *For no other foundation can anyone lay than that which is laid, which is Jesus Christ. Now if anyone builds on this foundation with gold, silver, precious stones, wood, hay, straw, each one's work will become manifest; for the Day will declare it, because it will be revealed by fire; and the fire will test each one's work, of what sort it is. If anyone's work which he has built on it endures, he will receive a reward. If anyone's work is burned, he will suffer loss; but he himself will be saved, yet so as through fire.*
>
> *1 Cor. 3:11–15*

Broken ropes allow the fire to purify us and allow us to know what Paul meant when he said we are crucified with Christ. It is like the hurt of the surgeon's knife which brings healing.

A friend made an interesting comment to me the other day. "There is a long term benefit for righteousness," he said, "and a short term benefit for sin. In other words, we have an immediate reward for sin and a long term price, and we have an immediate cost for righteousness and a long term pay back.

"Steve, if we received it all up front—if we got the benefit of righteousness quickly and paid the cost of sin right away—nobody would ever sin and everybody would be righteous."

His statement is not only insightful but also true of broken ropes. They hurt for the present, but the long term benefit is wonderful.

You Have a Fellow Sufferer

Finally, because God loves and values you, He has identified with you and has suffered from broken ropes too. The Bible says, "For we do not have a High Priest who cannot sympathize with our weaknesses, but was in all points tempted as we are, yet without sin" (Heb. 4:15).

Christ died not just to keep you from dying, but to die the way you must die; He suffered not to keep you from suffering, but to suffer just as you must suffer. He felt fear and temptation not just to keep you from feeling fear and temptation but to be afraid and tempted the way you are afraid and tempted. He experienced the loss of friends, family, and support, not just to keep you from that loss, but to lose friends, family, and support as you must lose them. Peter wrote, "For to this you were called, because Christ also suffered for us, leaving us an example, that you should follow His steps" (1 Pet. 2:21).

When Dr. Donald Grey Barnhouse served as a pastor in Philadelphia some enemies of the gospel were spreading slanderous stories about him. His attorney told Barnhouse that they would be able to take some legal action, "but," he said, "from now on when you hear these stories, you can't respond. You must always say, 'I cannot respond to that on the advice of my attorney.'"

You can imagine how difficult that was for Dr. Barnhouse. It's bad enough to hear untruths repeated about you, but it's horrible not to be able to respond to those untruths.

One day Barnhouse was walking down the street in Philadelphia when he met a fellow pastor. The pastor asked Dr. Barnhouse how he was doing, and Barnhouse told his friend about the slander and his visit to his attorney.

"Man!" the pastor said. "That must be terrible."

"Yes," Dr. Barnhouse replied, "it is very difficult."

"Your church must be ready to fire you."

"No," Barnhouse said. "As a matter of fact, my church has been wonderful. The elders of the church just gave me a raise and said, 'Pastor, we're doing this to let you know that we believe in you.'"

"Well, your family must be angry."

"No, they've been wonderful. During this time they have gone out of their way to express their love."

"Well, you must have lost friends."

"No," Dr. Barnhouse said. "I am fortunate in my friends. They have stood with me through all of this."

"Well, Donald," his friend said. "Have they driven nails through your hands and feet? Have they spit on you, and cursed you, and hung you on a cross?"

Dr. Barnhouse hung his head, finding something interesting in the crack in the sidewalk. He was obviously deep in thought.

Dr. Barnhouse's friend, not unkindly, said softly, "Donald, you have a long way to go yet to get to the cross."

4

How to Tie a Knot

*T*he Bible doesn't talk much about the reasons ropes break. If you have ever read the book of Job, you are aware that Job is not the place to go for answers to the problem of evil. The book of Job asks the question, If there is a good and loving God, why do our ropes break so much? And, by and large, the book doesn't provide answers to that question. And, except in general terms, neither does the rest of the Bible.

Although we don't always understand the reasons why our ropes break, they do. The question before us then is this: What do you do when the rope breaks?

The Means of Grace

I want to show you some of the ways God gives His grace—unmerited favor or help—to believers. The means of grace is the formal theological term for the ways God enables us to persevere in our salvation. Although I will not be speaking of the means of grace in the technical or restricted sense, the idea is the same. God is very practical, and He does not leave His people helpless.

In order to help you to understand the means of God's grace, I am going to preface each one with the adjective *honest*. If there is a problem Christians have in dealing with broken ropes, it's a problem with honesty. I certainly don't mean that Christians are outright dishonest. At least, most of the time we don't lie. But we often conceal untruths in spiritual language and pious platitudes. As a result, the truth gets lost in our maze of spiritualization.

We often hear non-Christians saying that they don't go to church because there are hypocrites in the church. That, of course, is nonsense. If you find sinners in the church, that is where they ought to be.

There are two kinds of people in the world: sinners who know they need God and sinners who don't know they need God. The first group (if they properly understand the Christian faith) are in the church. When pagans talk about hypocrisy, they usually refer to people who say being in the church makes them good. The fact is that if a person is a part of the church, he or she is proclaiming before the whole world that he or she is a sinner. The fact that Christians are sinners doesn't make Christians hypocrites. In reality, it proclaims the truth of the gospel.

However, people who are part of the church are hypocritical when they proclaim to each other that they are better, smarter, more spiritual, purer, and more loving than they really are. A healthy dose of honesty is one of the best things you can apply to breaking ropes. Let's talk about it.

Honest Prayer: Telling God the Truth

Honest prayer can really help when your rope has broken. One of the beautiful things about the psalms is their honesty with God. More often than not, the psalms constitute candid, straightforward prayers:

Save me, O God!
For the waters have come up to my neck.
I sink in deep mire,
Where there is no standing;
I have come into deep waters,
Where the floods overflow me.
I am weary with my crying;
My throat is dry;
My eyes fail while I wait for God.
Ps. 69:1–3

I remember the day it became apparent that I was going to have to withdraw from graduate school and give up my dream of being a pastor. It was a very difficult time. Anna and I were living in a slum apartment. She was pregnant, we had no money, and I was working two jobs just to keep us going. Tired and discouraged, I put Anna on a plane in Boston so she could go to visit her mother, and I headed toward the beaches of the North Shore. I didn't know much about God in those days, but I knew enough to know that I was hurt about my situation and angry at Him. I told Him so, too.

If you had been there you would have winced at the angry words which flowed from me as I shook my fist at God. I just didn't understand what He was doing. We were in a strange city, working with strange people, trying to do the impossible, "And You," I said to God, "have deserted us." That was about the softest thing I said to Him.

Later, as I began to learn about God the Father, I was ashamed at the things I had said. Still later, when I knew Him even better, I knew that the only Person in the world who could have understood my feelings was God and that I had gone to the right Person with them.

61

Did you know that there is a ministry of accepting bitterness? A young, beautiful, angry woman, she sat across from me and began to cry. The anger didn't show at first and perhaps the woman didn't even know she was angry.

"You have told me how badly your family and friends have treated you," I said. "You say you are hurt. I don't think you are hurt at all. I think you are very angry."

Her denial—"I am not!"—caught her off guard. Her next sentence was much softer. "I guess you're right," she said as she smiled through the tears. "That was a rather angry statement for someone who isn't angry."

During the next hour we began to look at some of the sources of her anger. The more she talked the more I realized that she was primarily angry at her sister.

"Why do you hate your sister?" I asked.

I was surprised at what came next. No one could be as bad as the sister she described. Throughout the outburst I remained silent. When she finished she said, "I wish she was dead!"

"Why?"

"Because," the young woman replied, "she is beautiful and good."

I saw that young woman a week later and she said to me, "Pastor, I feel so much better. I feel like the world is off my shoulders. I talked to my sister this morning and we are well on the way to reconciliation. Thank you for helping me express my bitterness."

Later, as I was praying about that situation, I realized God has the same kind of ministry with us, if we will only let Him. Most of the time it's impossible to express anger and bitterness to friends because they simply are not emotionally able to absorb or understand it. But God does understand.

If you are angry and hurt, don't tell God that you love Him. He knows you are lying. Don't tell Him that you know He is doing whatever He is doing in your life for a good reason. He knows you don't believe that for a moment. Tell Him the truth. He is maybe the only Person in the world Who can absorb everything you hand out, understand why you do it, and still love you.

Too often, when our ropes have broken, our prayers become spiritual nonsense. If we would stop talking nonsense for a moment, God would say to us, "Come off it! Tell me what you really think." Once we believers, who have had ropes break, understand that God can handle our honesty, the broken ropes don't seem as bad as they seemed before.

Honest Fellowship: Being Real with Each Other

Another means of grace, or help, God has given us is a community of believers who are honest with one another. Paul wrote to the Galatians to "Bear one another's burdens, and so fulfill the law of Christ" (Gal. 6:2).

We are often afraid, in the church, to tell people that our rope has broken lest they think that we aren't spiritual. We don't want people to know we're hurting because we fear that they'll think less of us. We remain silent when we are falling apart because we honestly believe Christians shouldn't fall apart.

As I write this, news of evangelists and political figures, caught in moral indiscretions, abound. The initial stories are tragic, the charges numerous—people caught yet paying for a number of years to keep others quiet. Each morning I pray particularly for those in the ministry who have fallen, not because I endorse their actions but because they are part of Christ's family. I pray for them because there is no sin I am not capable of committing. I pray for them because they and their supporters must be devastated. Because it hurts the members of the Body of Christ, it hurts me.

But do you know who I pray for the most? I pray for the Body of Christ that would create the kind of environment which requires other Christians to remain silent or to hide their sin by blackmail. I am not for a moment suggesting that every sin extant in our lives ought to be broadcast on television or confessed in church. (Did you hear about the priest listening to the rather long confession of one of his parishioners? The priest interrupted and said, "Son, stop it. You're not confessing; you're bragging.") However, I do believe that every Christian ought to have Christian friends before whom he or she can be totally honest.

I have a delightful friend who is sometimes devastatingly honest. I visited her in the hospital one time before she had surgery. I asked her if she was frightened, expecting to hear the general spiritual "stuff" I usually hear in response to that kind of question: "No, pastor, the Lord is faithful, and He has dealt with my fear." Instead I got one of the most honest answers I've ever heard from a Christian facing surgery. "Are you kidding? Of course I'm frightened," she exclaimed. "I'm scared to death. People die in this place!"

When your rope breaks, you need Christian brothers and sisters who are earthy enough to hear your fear, hurt, and sin without giving you some kind of spiritual party line. The church I serve is a very honest church. Often people who visit with us leave because they simply can't deal with the honesty.

The officers of the church had a retreat once without a speaker. We just wanted to get to know one another. One of the elders, who had a business in which he needed to be seen as successful, opened the retreat with these words, "Guys, I want you to know that my business is falling apart and I'm scared."

We spent most of the rest of the retreat ministering to him. Officers who had encountered similar business problems spoke to his problem; some just let him know they cared; still others started thinking of ways they could help him.

I had an agenda for that retreat. We were going to pray a lot, study the Scriptures a lot, and encourage each other a lot with spiritual songs. God had another agenda, and it started with this brother's honesty. We had not even had an opening prayer.

It's been awhile since that retreat, but one of the elders came to me recently and said, "Pastor, we need to have another retreat like the one when we all got honest." He had sensed something real at the retreat: the Spirit of God. When God's people are honest with one another, His Spirit is always present.

If you don't have brothers and sisters in Christ with whom you can be less than "spiritual," find some.

Honest Bible Study: Reading Beyond the "Spiritual"

The third means of grace which can make a difference when your rope breaks is honest Bible study. I don't know where in the world we got the idea that the

Bible was a "spiritual" book. (When I use the word *spiritual* I am, of course, not talking about God and His Kingdom, but about false religious trappings.) It isn't. It is honest, earthy, and practical. Before I learned to love the Bible, I wanted to love the Bible. I thought I would love the Bible because it was so "spiritual," and I honestly was trying to love "spiritual" things.

I have been walking with Christ for many years now. I'm a Bible teacher, and I love the Bible. However, I love the Bible not because it's "spiritual" but because it's so honest and real.

I don't know about you, but I'm tired of people lying to me. I bought a car once from a man who promised that their business's service was better than their car. "Our car is the best in the industry," he said, "and our service is even better." After months of trying to communicate my problems to the service people, I finally called the customer service headquarters. Do you know what happened? They didn't even answer the phone! Can you believe that? When I think about it, it still makes me very angry.

In that kind of world—the world where it is common practice to lie—it's wonderful to go someplace where I know I'll hear the truth. That place is Scripture. When God gave us the Bible, He didn't sugar-coat what He had to say; I'm glad He didn't make the Bible a public relations piece. When my rope breaks, I don't need that.

The Bible presents great men and women of God doing very ungodly things. You'll find dishonesty, adultery, fear, bitterness, and discouragement coming from the saints. I didn't understand that when I started reading the Bible. But the more I read, the more I realized that God wanted us to see real people trying to deal with broken ropes. But God wanted to do more than that; He wanted us to see "the whole picture." The Bible not only portrays the lives of people who, like us, dealt with broken ropes but also it shows us the best way to deal with broken ropes—that is, we can change the situation if possible, and if not, we accept it with grace and power.

I love the comment that when we read the Bible we ought to read those portions we have *not* underlined. Underlining is a good practice, but it can hurt your Bible study. If you've had your Bible for a long time and have done a lot of underlining, get a "fresh" one. You will be amazed at the things God said that you haven't underlined.

Honest Action: Doing What Needs Doing

Another means of grace God has given us is honest action. The Bible is not a passive book. Scripture challenges us to run the race, to fight the fight, to wrestle with angelic powers (1 Cor. 9:24, 27; Eph. 6:12). The let-go-and-let-God philosophy may be good in some situations, but in others it is absolutely wrong. We need to be still sometimes, but sometimes we simply need to get busy and do what needs doing.

The prophet Elijah is one of my favorite biblical characters. After one of his great victories for God, he was chased by the enemy of God, Jezebel. After all of the great things he had done, his rope broke. Scripture says that Elijah went into the wilderness and had a pity party. He prayed, "It is enough! Now, LORD, take my life, for I am no better than my fathers!" (1 Kings 19:4).

Have you ever felt like that? That is one of the normal, human ways we deal with broken ropes: We just want to die. When we lose our job, go through a divorce, suffer major financial loss, lose a loved one, our first re-action is often apathy and depression. We want to go away and do nothing. Sometimes, however, we should act.

In 1 Kings the story of Elijah's pity party continues:

> *Then as he lay and slept under a broom tree, suddenly an angel touched him, and said to him, "Arise and eat." Then he looked, and there by his head was a cake baked on coals, and a jar of water. So he ate and drank, and lay down again. And the angel of the LORD came back the second time, and touched him, and said, "Arise and eat, because the journey is too great for you." So he arose, and ate and drank; and he went in the strength of that food forty days and forty nights as far as Horeb, the mountain of God.*
>
> 1 Kings 19:5–8

Elijah had decided that he would go no further, but God had a different plan. There are, of course, times when you can do nothing more about your broken rope, and we'll talk about that in a moment. However, you must be very sure that there is nothing more to do before you decide not to act.

When you place your hand on a hot stove, your hand doesn't hurt because you haven't prayed enough or been spiritual enough. Your hand hurts because it's on a hot stove. Don't pray. Take your hand off the stove.

If you've lost your job, get busy and look for another one. If you've broken your leg, get a cast. If you've gone through a divorce, get on about the business of living. If you've lost a loved one, grieve and then start living. If you have sinned, ask forgiveness and get out of the mud.

Amazingly, the remedy for a broken rope is often a pep talk. Early in my ministry I spent most of my counseling time sympathizing with people whose rope had broken. Now, there's nothing wrong with sympathy, but there's a lot wrong with too much sympathy. Too much sympathy can debilitate a Christian.

Sometimes I'll say to people (as it was said to me when my rope was broken and I was looking for sympathy), "All right now, it's time to grow up. You know what has happened; you know why it has happened; you've had your pity party. What are you going to do about it now?" Sometimes these words are greeted with anger. Sometimes the person says, "You simply don't understand what I'm going through." I often acknowledge that I don't. "But you are going through it," I'll say, "and since you are, you have to do something about it. If you are looking for more sympathy, go to your mother."

Harsh? Yes, but sometimes harshness is love. Because I have brothers and sisters in Christ who have loved me enough to be harsh with me, I have learned to love others enough to be harsh with them. Sometimes the best remedy for a broken rope is to tie a knot and (mixing the metaphor) to keep on trucking.

Honest Relinquishment: Accepting What God Gives You

The fifth means of grace is honest relinquishment. The book of Job gives an amazing illustration of relinquishment. Job had just received the news that he had lost everything: his fortune was gone and his children were dead.

> *Then Job arose and tore his robe and shaved his head,*
> *And he fell to the ground and worshiped*
> *And he said: "Naked I came from my mother's womb,*

69

And naked shall I return there.
The LORD *gave, and the* LORD *has taken away;*
Blessed be the name of the LORD."

Job 1:20–21

Later Job was inflicted with painful boils all over his body. To make matters worse, his wife then said to him,

"Do you still hold to your integrity? Curse God and die!" But he said to her, "You speak as one of the foolish women speaks. Shall we indeed accept good from God, and shall we not accept adversity?" In all this Job did not sin with his lips.

Job 2:9–10

I heard a comic say the other day that the Talmud, the collection of Jewish law, taught that where there is no solution there is no problem. If there isn't a solution, you don't have a problem. Instead, you have a fact. About the only thing you can do with a fact is accept it. As one friend of mine says, "If you can't fight it or flee from it, flow with it." That's good advice but it's not complete.

The Bible is not fatalistic. God does not want us to say about our broken rope, "Well, that's life. My rope broke; I'll just have to accept it." God has ordained the events of lives; and if He ordains our lives and He is loving (which He is), then Romans 8:28 is true: "And we know that all things work together for good to those who love God, to those who are the called according to His purpose."

The principle is *positive relinquishment:* Whenever something comes into your life that you cannot change or avoid, accept it as coming from the hand of your loving Father. Do you have to like it? Of course not. I can't stand spinach or okra, but when my wife fixes it, I eat it because, I am told, it's good for me. I never have understood why God didn't make the things that are good for you taste good, and the things that are bad for you taste bad. A lot of people say that when they get to heaven they're going to ask God about the major perplexities of life. I just want to know why God made spinach taste so bad and why God would cause something as hairy and slick as okra to be packed with vitamins.

When your rope breaks and you can do nothing about making the fall better, accept it as having been ordained by God. When author Catherine Marshall went to Washington with her pastor husband, Peter, to serve one of the most prominent Presbyterian churches in the country, she became sick and bedridden. She did everything in her power to get well. She saw doctors, she took her medicine, and she prayed for healing. Do you know what happened? She stayed sick.

She then decided that she was sick because of sin and promptly began to write everyone she could think of whom she had ever wronged to ask forgiveness. She even wrote a grammar-school teacher, because she had, while in that teacher's class, looked at the paper of another student during a test. Do you know what happened? She stayed sick.

After that, she got really angry at God. She told Him she really didn't like what He was doing to her and demanded that He change the situation. Do you know what happened? She stayed sick.

Finally, in desperation, Catherine Marshall fell back on her bed and prayed, "Lord, You know I don't like myself the way I am. I am the wife of a busy pastor and he needs me. I have done everything I can to get well, and I'm still sick. Lord, I belong to You, and if this is the way You want me to be the rest of my life, that is Your right. I relinquish my health to You trusting that You know what You are doing." Do you know what happened? From that moment she started getting better.

Now I would not say, nor does the Bible teach, that when you relinquish your broken rope you won't have the problem anymore. However, sometimes that does happen. And if it doesn't, relinquish that to Him too. Positive relinquishment might not be a solution to your problem, but it can help you deal with it.

Honest Victory: Celebrating When You Get Things Right

The final means of grace I want you to remember when your rope breaks is honest victory. Not only was Paul honest when he messed up, but he was also honest when he did things right. After speaking about his intense struggle with sin, Paul wrote, "O wretched man that I am! Who will deliver me from this body of death? I thank God—through Jesus Christ our Lord!" (Rom. 7:24–25). On the other hand I love Paul's call to the Philippians: "Brethren, join in following my example, and note those who so walk, as you have us for a pattern" (Phil. 3:17). Was that pride? No. It was honesty.

One of the problems with honesty about your failure and sin is that it can become addictive. You can think that the only real honesty is honesty about failure. If you are honest about your failure, be just as honest about your success.

A lot of Christians are not walking properly before the Lord because they have used the excuse that they aren't like some pastor or religious leader. "Well, he or she is a saint," they say. "If I were a saint, I would be more obedient." Pastors shouldn't be put on spiritual pedestals. They ought to be considered just as human as anyone else. I want to be honest with you about the places where I fall apart, because I want you to be encouraged and inspired about the places where I'm getting things together. I want you to do the same thing for me.

I went through a period in my Bible teaching when I was so upset at the idea of people accepting Christianity without a cross that all I did was warn believers that we weren't home yet and that they couldn't expect to receive God's promises about heaven now. I preached over and over again that we lived in a fallen world where, when you get 51 percent right, you can file it under success.

One of the elders in the church I serve said to me, "Pastor, you have taught us that even truth, when taught to the exclusion of other truth, can become a lie. If someone had heard you teach only over the past few weeks they would think that you don't believe God answers prayer, that people are healed, and that Christians can live victorious and joyful lives." I thought about what he said and the next Sunday began correcting some of the wrong impressions I had left with the congregation.

Because we are talking about broken ropes in this book, we need to talk about the realities of failure, sin, tragedy, and relinquishment. However, I don't want you to think that's the whole story. God still answers prayer; He still mends broken ropes.

When Jesus told Peter that Peter was going to deny Him, Jesus didn't stop there. He said a very compassionate and beautiful thing to Peter. Jesus said, "Simon, Simon! Indeed, Satan has asked for you, that he may sift you as wheat. But I have prayed for you, that your faith should not fail; and when you have returned to Me, strengthen your brethren" (Luke 22:31–32).

He says the same thing to you as you are dealing with your broken rope. When things get better, don't waste a bit of what you're going through. Take what you learn from your broken rope, and help those who are still in the thick of it.

That may be the reason your rope broke in the first place.

5

The Bane of Bitterness

Sartre's play, *The Flies*, an adaptation of Aeschylus's story of Orestes, depicts a conversation between Zeus, king of the gods, and Orestes, whom Zeus considered dangerous. Orestes told Zeus that he would no longer bow to Zeus. Electra, Orestes's sister, pleaded with Orestes not to add blasphemy to his crime.

"Mark her words, young man," Zeus said. "And hope no more to win her back by arguments like these. Such language is somewhat new to her ears, and somewhat shocking."

"To my ears, too," Orestes replied. "And to my lungs, which breathe the words, and to my tongue, which shapes them. In fact, I can hardly understand myself. Only yesterday you were still a veil on my eyes, a clot of wax in my ears; yesterday, indeed, I had an excuse. You were my excuse for being alive, for you had put me in the world to fulfill your purpose, and the world was an old pander prating to me about your goodness, day in, day out. And then you forsook me."

"I forsook you? How?"

"Yesterday, when I was with Electra, I felt at one with Nature, this Nature of your making. It sang the praises of the Good—your Good—in siren tones, and lavished intimations. To lull me into gentleness, the fierce light mellowed and grew tender as a lover's eyes.

And, to teach me the forgiveness of offenses, the sky grew bland as a pardoner's face. Obedient to your will, my youth rose up before me and pleaded with me like a girl who fears her lover will forsake her. That was the last time, the last, I saw my youth. Suddenly, out of the blue, freedom crashed down on me and swept me off my feet. Nature sprang back, my youth went with the wind, and I knew myself alone, utterly alone in the midst of this well-meaning little universe of yours. I was like a man who's lost his shadow. And there was nothing left in heaven, no right or wrong, nor anyone to give me orders."[1]

Orestes's declaration of autonomy was the last refuge of a bitter pagan. This kind of existentialism is not a positive philosophy, for Orestes's autonomy did not lead to peace. However, Sartre was too honest to write into his play a happy ending.

No Escape from the Truth

Believers don't have the option of autonomy. As St. Teresa of Avila said, once one has seen the truth, it's hard to unsee it. Once we see God's sovereignty, it's hard to claim autonomy.

A minister who was quite unbelieving in his theology had attended a very liberal seminary and had bought the "party" line, the group's philosophy. When he started to pastor a church, he found out that what he had been taught simply didn't work. Seminaries that rob their students of the foundational truths of the Christian faith rob them of the spiritual, psychological, and motivational reasons for maintaining the institution (the church) they were called to serve. When this minister brought the unbelief he had learned in seminary to the church, he found out what most people with common sense already knew: If the Christian faith isn't true, there is no earthly reason to maintain the church built around Christian principles. The pastor found that not only did the congregation need the Christian truths but also that he needed them. Forgiveness, meaning, and truth were necessary for his own survival.

Over a period of months I met with this minister, and he began to see Christ as revealed in the Bible as the foundation of the church. He also began to put into practice what he had learned. He held a revival in his church and invited a strong, Bible-believing evangelist to speak. He printed up brochures and spread them all over town, and he urged his congregation to be involved.

I would like to tell you that, because of his faithfulness, thousands were saved and hundreds were healed. But that isn't what happened. Not one single person came to the first service.

My friend began to suffer from physical problems which had emotional roots. Twice he was taken to the hospital because he thought he was suffering from a coronary, but there was no indication whatsoever of a heart problem. He was about as welcome in his church as a wet shaggy dog shaking himself at a Miss America pageant. People in the church wanted the same old liberal, superficial pap. When my friend began to teach the Bible the church didn't like it one bit.

One day my pastor friend came into my study absolutely devastated. As soon as the door was shut, he began to sob. "Steve," he cried, "it's all coming apart. I wish I had never found out the truth." I asked him if he was going to turn away from what he'd been learning, and I'll never forget his answer. He said through his tears, "No, I would like to run away from the whole thing, but I've gone too far to get out."

The problem with being a thinking Christian is once you see the truth, you can't ever get away from it. You can't deny the reality of what you have experienced and understood. You can't deny that God loves you and has ordained the events of your life. It becomes a very perplexing situation.

Listen to Job's words as he faced that dilemma. He had gone through a wrenching time in his life. Every rope that ever held him had broken, and he knew God. The bitterness with which he spoke was cutting:

> *"How then can I answer Him,*
> *And choose my words to reason with Him?*
> *For though I were righteous, I could not answer Him;*
> *I would beg mercy of my Judge.*
> *If I called and He answered me,*
> *I would not believe that He was listening to my voice.*
> *For He crushes me with a tempest, and multiplies my*
> *   wounds without cause.*
> *He will not allow me to catch my breath,*
> *But fills me with bitterness."*
>
> Job 9:14–18

If you've ever been in Job's place, you know his problem. You're caught with no place to go for recourse. There is no court where you can plead your case. There is nothing you can do. You stand with your broken rope in your hand, and all you can do is hurt. You'd like to run away, to deny the reality you've known, but that simply isn't a viable alternative.

Dear friend, that is the stuff of which bitterness is made. Let's talk about it.

The Root of Bitterness

I suspect the first thing we ought to do is define the disease before we look for a cure. Hebrews 12:15 says not to allow any root of bitterness springing up to cause trouble. The "root of bitterness" refers to Deuteronomy 29:18:

> So that there may not be among you man or woman or family or tribe, whose heart turns away today from the LORD our God, to go and serve the gods of these nations, and that there may not be among you a root bearing bitterness or wormwood.

Bitterness comes from our turning away from the true God, and it has tremendous social implications. Bitterness—characterized by feelings of hatred, envy, resentment, cynicism, and severity—begins when one turns from God, and it results in a disease that infects others.

But the question is, How does one avoid bitterness?

In the next few pages I want to talk to two kinds of people. First, I want to talk to those of you whose rope has not broken. To you I would speak a word of preparation. Then, I want to have some time with those of you whose rope has already broken. Perhaps you are already dealing with bitterness. To you I want to speak a word of healing.

Someone has said that life is the only school where you take the test and then learn the lesson. That sounds good, and in some cases I suppose it's true, but it isn't the way God works with breaking ropes. You can learn the lessons about broken ropes before you take the test. And if you can learn the lessons, you can avoid the bitterness which often follows the test. The following three lessons are hedges against the bane of bitterness and presuppose that you have a personal relationship to Christ.

Prayer before You Panic

The first lesson you can learn before the exam is the lesson of *prayer before the panic*. Make sure your relationship with God is strong so that, when the rope breaks, you will have built a foundation of faith. I call it being prayed up.

Daniel is a great example of someone who was faithful to God both before and after a crisis. King Darius, at the instigation of his own stooges, plotted to get rid of Daniel. They figured that the best thing to do was to issue a proclamation which would require everyone in the kingdom to worship Darius.

> *So these governors and satraps thronged before the king, and said thus to him: "King Darius, live forever! All the governors of the kingdom, the administrators and satraps, the counselors and advisors, have consulted together to establish a royal statute and to make a firm decree, that whoever petitions any god or man for thirty days, except you, O king, shall be cast into the den of lions."*
>
> *Daniel 6:6–7*

It was a masterful stroke of genius. The king was flattered, and Daniel was doomed. Darius signed the decree, and the king's leaders figured they had finally found a way to get rid of Daniel. They were right, and they were wrong.

Now when Daniel knew that the writing was signed, he went home. And in his upper room, with his windows open toward Jerusalem, he knelt down on his knees three times that day, and prayed and gave thanks before his God, as was his custom since early days.

Daniel 6:10, emphasis added

You know the rest of the story. Daniel ended up in the lion's den, but the lions weren't hungry.

The story of Daniel is not given to us to illustrate how God delivers people from lions. The story shows how a man of God should face lions. Because Daniel had prayed regularly long before he faced the lions, Daniel did not become bitter. Daniel's ministry spanned the entire horrible seventy-year period of the Babylonian captivity of God's people. You would expect Daniel to have been bitter. And yet, in the midst of the slavery and the destruction, you find in Daniel an incredible hope and power. When you see Daniel's demeanor before he faced the lions, you know why.

A farmer and his son were working in the fields when they looked up and saw a tornado coming in their direction. The farmer threw down his hoe and started running toward the farmhouse. When he looked back over his shoulder he saw that his son had fallen on his knees and was praying. "Son," the farmer shouted, "don't pray. Run. A scared prayer ain't worth a dime."

Well, a scared prayer is worth more than that. But a prayer prayed in the quiet before the storm is worth a lot more. Now is the time to draw near to God so when the

81

rope breaks, you will have a solid relationship which will prevent the horror of bitterness. Too many Christians pray only in storms. I suppose it's better to pray in storms than not to pray at all. But God's call is for a daily walk with Him, which prepares you for the test when it comes.

Knowledge before the Kick-off

The second lesson a Christian ought to learn before the rope breaks and bitterness follows is *knowledge before the kickoff*. The writer of Proverbs said, "The heart of the prudent acquires knowledge, / And the ear of the wise seeks knowledge" (Prov. 18:15).

The Christian life is a lot like being in school. It took me a long time to understand how to study in college, but when I did learn I began to make good grades. I found that cramming for an exam didn't work. If I didn't know it by the night before the exam, I probably wasn't going to learn it. So I learned to study regularly throughout the course, and the night before the exam I simply reviewed what I already knew.

One of our great problems as believers is that some of us think nothing bad will happen to us when we begin to follow Christ. Some feel that God is in the business of preventing tragedy and are devastated when their ropes break. They become bitter. You see, they have not prepared themselves by learning sound doctrine and studying the Bible seriously. Disney-World Christianity may work in a world where everything is clean and fun and right. But it simply won't work in a world where there is disease, death, and heartbreak. You've got to have a tough faith for a tough world.

The apostle Peter spent a considerable amount of time warning believers of the trials they must face. Then he said, "Therefore gird up the loins of your mind, be sober, and rest your hope fully upon the grace that is to be brought to you at the revelation of Jesus Christ" (1 Pet. 1:13). "Beloved," he wrote, "do not think it strange concerning the fiery trial which is to try you, as though some strange thing happened to you" (1 Pet. 4:12).

One of the things I've noticed in my years as a pastor is that most people die in the same way they have lived. We hear a lot about "deathbed conversions," but to be perfectly honest with you, those conversions are few and far between. You would think that one would get it right with God as one would "cram for finals." However, most people who would have nothing to do with God during their lives, will have nothing to do with Him in their last moments. If a person blasphemes during his or her life, he or she will probably blaspheme just before death. Those who have had a mild concern for God during their lives have a mild concern for God as they are dying. I can't tell you how many times I've heard people say, "I cared nothing for God during my life, and I will not be a hyprocrite now."

But it isn't just in matters of death where one's colors remain the same. Let me give you a principle: Most people react to breaking ropes in the same way they react to ropes that don't break. In other words, if you are faithful, loving, and obedient when things are going right in your life, you will probably be faithful, loving, and obedient when things are going wrong.

Bob Griese, former quarterback for the Miami Dolphins, was not known for his great physical prowess. Bob's mind made him great. When the defense was on the field, Bob was sitting on the bench, studying his play book. He didn't learn the game of football after the kick-off. He knew it in his head before he played it on the field. Similarly, you can allow the Bible to teach you about breaking ropes before yours breaks. Then, when it breaks, you will live out what you've learned.

Bitterness results from expecting the rope to hold. If you expect it to hold and it breaks, you are apt to be surprised and also bitter. Knowledge is the lesson before the exam.

Thanks before the Tragedy

The third lesson in preventing bitterness is *thanks before the tragedy*. The apostle Paul wrote,

> *And do not be drunk with wine, in which is dissipation; but be filled with the Spirit, speaking to one another in psalms and hymns and spiritual songs, singing and making melody in your heart to the Lord,* giving thanks always for all things to God the Father in the name of our Lord Jesus Christ.
> *Ephes. 5:18–20, emphasis added*

David O'Dowd was once teaching in a church where I was pastor. Dave said that the admonishment to give thanks for all things meant that we are to thank God for the apparent good *and* the apparent bad: both are from the hand of God.

Job thanked God for all things, at least at the beginning of his tragedy. You remember that Job's wife had had enough of all of their problems, and she suggested that Job simply curse God and die. Job's answer was straight and to the point: "You speak as one of the foolish women speaks. Shall we indeed accept good from God, and shall we not accept adversity?" (Job 2:10).

When Dave had finished teaching, he asked for questions. A man raised his hand and asked, "Do you mean that we are to thank God for tragedy and death?"

"Well," Dave said, "I don't like giving thanks for tragedy and death, but I have a question: Do you have an alternative?"

The alternatives were, of course, not very good. One could believe that God had nothing to do with this world's tragedies and that things were simply out of control. One could believe that God was a monster and rail against Him. One could believe that God was basically good but helpless. All of those alternatives led to bitterness. The only alternative which wouldn't lead to bitterness was the recognition that everything that came from the hand of the Father was proper and should be received with praise and thanksgiving.

In the early seventeenth century, one of the Scottish Covenanters was in jail waiting for his execution when his son's head was brought to him on a platter. He fell back to the ground, stricken beyond belief with the cruelty of his oppressors. Then he picked himself up and very softly said, "It is the Lord. Good is the will of the Lord."

Understanding that everything comes from God and praising Him for it is an effective way to prevent bitterness. Learn to thank God in the little things like traffic jams, late appointments, crying children, angry husbands, and burnt toast. Then when the rope really breaks you will have established a hedge against bitterness.

Let me say a word about some of the writings on the subject of praising God in all things. A number of books suggest or imply that if one learns to praise God in all things, all things will work out to one's liking. I wish that were true, but it isn't. An attitude of praise will grant you power *under* pressure, but power without pressure is never promised by God.

When You Aren't Prepared

If you have not exercised the lessons of prayer before the panic, knowledge before the kickoff, and thanks before the tragedy, and your rope breaks, then what do you do?

Recognizing the Effects of Bitterness

Recognize the horrible effect of bitterness. You've heard that bitterness only hurts the one who is bitter. It does, but it doesn't stop there. A person's bitterness infects everyone who comes into contact with him or her. Do you remember Gollum in J. R. R. Tolkein's trilogy, *The Lord of the Rings?* Gollum had once touched the ring but had lost it. The event ruined his life, and he became a pitiful, bitter, hateful creature. Toward the end of the trilogy, Sam and Frodo are on their way to destroy the ring when Gollum attacks them. In the scene you can see the stark reality of bitterness, depicted in terms of demon possession, selfishness, and destruction. Gollum is about to lose the ring forever, and his hatred knows no bounds.

> A sudden weight smote him and he crashed forward, tearing the backs of his hands that still clasped his master's. Then he knew what had happened, for above him as he lay he heard a hated voice.
> "Wicked masster!" it hissed. "Wicked masster cheats us; cheats Smeagol, gollum. He mustn't go that

way. He musstn't hurt Precious. Give it to Smeagol, yess, give it to us! Give it to uss!"

With a violent heave Sam rose up. At once he drew his sword; but he could do nothing. Gollum and Frodo were locked together. Gollum was tearing at his master, trying to get at the chain and the Ring. This probably was the only thing that could have roused the dying embers of Frodo's heart and will: an attack, an attempt to wrest his treasure from him by force. He fought back with a sudden fury that amazed Sam, and Gollum also. Even so things might have gone far otherwise, if Gollum himself had remained unchanged; but whatever dreadful paths, lonely and hungry and waterless, he had trodden, driven by a devouring desire and a terrible fear, they had left grievous marks on him. He was a lean, starved, haggard thing, all bones and tight-drawn sallow skin. A wild light flamed in his eyes, but his malice was no longer matched by his old griping strength.[2]

Bitterness is often called righteous indignation, demanding one's rights, or legitimate anger. But it is none of those. It is a black, horrible, debilitating disease. It will kill you and others.

Do you remember in Homer's *Odyssey*, when Ulysses (i.e., Odysseus) and his men were sailing past the island of the two Sirens, who sang the song of death? Ulysses had his men place wax in their ears and strap him to the mast so that he could enjoy the Sirens' song.

"Come here," they sang, "renowned Ulysses, honour to the Achaean name, and listen to our two voices. No one ever sailed past us without staying to hear the enchanting sweetness of our song—and he who listens will go on his way not only charmed, but wiser, for we know all the ills that the gods laid upon the Argives and

Trojans before Troy, and can tell you everything that is going to happen over the whole world."

They sang these words most musically, and as I longed to hear them further I made signs by frowning to my men that they should set me free; but they quickened their stroke, and Eurylochus and Perimedes bound me with still stronger bonds till we had got out of hearing of the Sirens' voices. Then my men took the wax from their ears and unbound me.[3]

Bitterness is like the song of the Sirens—extremely attractive but lethal. The Christian psychiatrist James Mallory said that many of us have our emotional "hall of injustice," and we like to visit it often. We like to polish the statues of those who have hurt us. We like to mull over all of those incidents where we were treated unfairly and unjustly. We like to bask in the sweet Siren song of bitterness, planning the ways we will get even.

If your rope is broken, make sure you recognize the horror of bitterness and then, with an act of your will, reject it.

Confessing the Tendency Toward Bitterness

Confess your tendency toward bitterness. Confess the reality of your nature to God. Tell Him that you are "ticked" and that you want to be bitter. Even tell Him that you think you have a right to be bitter. Then ask for His forgiveness. John wrote, "If we confess our sins, He is faithful and just to forgive us our sins and to cleanse us from all unrighteousness" (1 John 1:9).

Confession is not only good for the soul but also for the attitude. In my prayer list I have a special section called the Hit List. I determine to confess before God those people and incidents that make me angry and bitter. The more I confess and pray about those incidents, the smaller the list becomes. No one is on that list now because I am willing to confess the problem before the Father and allow Him to do what I can't do—remove the bitterness.

Exercising Relinquishment

Further, learn to exercise the principle of relinquishment: What we relinquish to God, He accepts and changes. We spoke of positive relinquishment in the last chapter, but there is more. To be perfectly honest, you can't turn bitterness on and off like a faucet. Bitterness is hard to destroy. God's Spirit must be given the freedom to act, and He can't act in you without your permission.

Paul wrote, "Let all bitterness . . . be put away from you" (Eph. 4:31). That's hard. But God gives us the power to do what He tells us to do.

We ought to pray: "Father, here I sit with my broken rope and I'm angry. Bitterness wells up in me, and I don't know what to do about it or even if I *want* to do anything about it. I now take the situation I don't like, and I give it to You. You deal with the situation as You see fit, and You deal with me as You see fit. I trust You to give me an explanation when I get to heaven, if I need one." That kind of prayer is dynamite, and through such prayer God can give you a brand new attitude about your broken rope.

Waiting for the Light

Finally, just be still and wait for the light of God's grace and presence to shine. Don't make what I've said into a step-by-step system whereby you "fix" bitterness though. It doesn't work that way.

If God is sovereign (and He is) and if He loves you (and He does) and if you have done everything you can (and sometimes you have), then don't do anything more. Simply be still.

I had a friend who refused to take drugs to dull his senses when he was dying. "Steve," he said, "all of my life I have faced whatever God has given, accepted it, and experienced the depth of whatever He, from His loving hand, has meted out. I want to experience death in the same way. It scares me, but what scares me more is that I should die without knowing and experiencing the fullness of death. Don't let them give me drugs that dull my senses."

That was an extremely brave thing to say. But in his braveness, there was redemption. He was still, and he accepted what God had given. His death was a release of great joy; there was a light on his face I have rarely seen on the face of one who had suffered and died.

Jesus' final shout on the cross was, "It is finished!" (John 19:30). That was a shout of relief and joy. Among other things, He was saying, "I have faced and experienced all that the Father has given, and praise the Father, it is over." You see, when you are hanging on a cross you can hardly do anything except hang on the cross. The nails won't let you get off, and the pain won't let you cover it with clichés. Crosses, though excruciatingly painful, provide some of the greatest joy in this world once they are accepted and experienced.

A couple of years ago my wife and I went through some of the most trying weeks of our lives. There were a number of deaths in our family, we were going through some serious financial problems, and the roof started leaking. Do you know what we did? We started laughing. If you had been there, you would have thought we had lost our minds. We laughed until tears rolled down our faces. Here we were suffering to the depth of our being, and we were laughing. It wasn't bitter laughter, nor was it the laughter of cynicism. It was a free and freeing laughter.

So much bad was happening and there was so little we could do about it that the whole episode became funny in a twisted sort of way. When we had finished laughing we noted a difference. Our situation was still as bad as it had been before. Nothing had changed . . . except us.

Satan hated our laughter. He had some plans that were thwarted by it. He wanted to make us bitter. But because the laughter reflected our acceptance of our broken rope, it made him bitter.

Better him than us.

6

Where Did I Go Wrong?

A friend of mine often says in a kidding fashion, "Steve, of course I'm right. I'm always right. . . . except for one time when I thought I was wrong."

Too many Christians, though, think they are wrong. Someone has said that if a swarm of locusts attacked a third-world country causing a famine, the Christians would ask, "Where did I go wrong?" Because we think we are wrong, it is easy for us to believe that, when our rope breaks, we are being punished for our wrong.

The point of the book of Job is that the explanations Job's friends offered attributing his problems to his sin were dead wrong. Job had done nothing wrong. He had not turned his back on God. He was not out of the will of God. He had not done anything stupid. He was not being chastened by God. He had not offended God. Job, you see, was the victim of a world where bad stuff happens. And Job knew that the bad stuff happening to him was not the result of his sin:

> *"I am blameless, yet I do not know myself;*
> *I despise my life.*
> *It is all one thing;*
> *Therefore I say, 'He destroys the blameless and the wicked.'*
> *If the scourge slays suddenly,*

He laughs at the plight of the innocent,
The earth is given into the hand of the wicked.
He covers the faces of its judges.
If it is not He, who else could it be?"

Job 9:21-24

Now, the words of Job weren't very spiritual. His bitterness was harsh, and his words were angry. But Job's saying "I am blameless"was the absolute truth of the book.

Job's friend Zophar, however, subscribed to the doctrine of divine earthly retribution—that is, he believed that people are rewarded for doing good and punished for doing evil. When Job said that he had done nothing wrong, Zophar replied,

"Know therefore that God exacts from you
Less than your iniquity deserves.
. . . .
If you would prepare your heart,
And stretch out your hands toward Him;
If iniquity were in your hand, and you put it far away,
And would not let wickedness dwell in your tents;
. . . .
. . . you would forget your misery,
And remember it as waters that have passed away,
And your life would be brighter than noonday."

Job 11:6, 13-14, 16-17

A lot of us, like Zophar, believe that when we are good, we are rewarded and when we are bad, we are punished. Is that really true? If your rope has broken, does that mean you have done something wrong and are being punished?

Have I Done Something Wrong?

Do you ever read novels and skip ahead to find out what happens? Sometimes the temptation to find out the end is overwhelming, and if you are that kind of person, you will be tempted to turn ahead and find out the answer to the question posed above. Don't do it! Let me tell you the answer to the question here so you won't skip the process between here and there. The answer is: Not necessarily. In other words, there is no direct absolute correlation between breaking ropes and breaking God's law. Your rope can break and you may not have done anything wrong at all.

The Chastening Rope

First, you need to know that broken ropes can sometimes be the result of God's chastening. God does sometimes allow us to experience broken ropes so that we can learn valuable lessons. The writer of Hebrews said "'For whom the LORD loves He chastens, / And scourges every son whom He receives'" (Heb. 12:6).

Sometimes ropes break because God is treating us the way a father treats his child. Have you ever been around spoiled children? Their parents threaten to discipline them, but they never follow through. They say, "Billy, if you do that one more time, I'm going to spank you." Of course, Billy tries it just one more time to check it out. He figures it's worth a spanking just to see if his parents are telling the truth. Then the father or mother says, "Billy, did you hear me? If you do that again, you are going to get the spanking of your life." By this time, Billy knows that his parents won't spank him, so he does whatever he wants.

Everybody else tries to be tolerant. "After all," people say, "he isn't my child." But as time wears on and Billy gets louder and more obnoxious, I want to say, "Look, if you aren't going to punish that kid, let me do it. I would consider it a high and holy privilege to smack that kid, just once."

Have you heard about the man who was in a supermarket with his little boy? As they went up and down the aisles, the little boy was causing havoc by pulling produce off the shelves and making piles of the produce on the floor. Over and over, the man muttered, "Now Tommy, be calm. Don't do it. Don't do it. Be calm, Tommy."

Finally, the manager of the store came to the man and said, "Sir, you must control Tommy. Words simply aren't enough."

"You don't understand," the man said, "He's Sam. I'm Tommy."

Well, God isn't like the parents of these two boys. God is sovereign; He is loving; and He is our Father. His discipline is sometimes harsh because He has a plan for us, and His plan will not be thwarted. Do you know what His plan is? "Beloved, now we are children of God; and it has not yet been revealed what we shall be, but we know that when He is revealed, we shall be like Him, for we shall see Him as He is" (1 John 3:2).

How about that? Someday you are going to be like Jesus. That's a great miracle! The problem for all of us is getting from here to there. If you think that's going to be easy, you're crazy. It's going to take a lot of sandpaper and a lot of chiseling and a lot of hammering. God's sandpaper, chisels, and hammers are our broken ropes—sometimes.

A Dumb Mistake

Secondly, ropes sometimes break because we do something stupid. Do you remember when Moses was telling Pharaoh to let the people of Israel go, and God sent a plague of frogs? Now I don't mean just a few frogs. I'm talking lots and lots of frogs. Moses told Pharaoh, "If you refuse to let them go, behold, I will smite all your territory with frogs. So the river shall bring forth frogs abundantly" (Exod. 8:2–3). That's exactly what happened.

Pharaoh is up to his ears in frogs. He is eating frog bread and frog soup. Everywhere he walks, he is stepping on frogs. When he sleeps at night there is the squish feeling of frogs in his bed.

Here is the amazing part of that story. Pharaoh, not surprisingly, told Moses that if Moses would get rid of the frogs, Pharaoh would allow the people of God to leave. "And Moses said to Pharaoh, 'Accept the honor of saying when I shall intercede for you, for your servants, and for your people, to destroy the frogs from you and your houses, that they may remain in the river only.'" So he said, "Tomorrow" (Exod. 8:9–10). Can you believe that? Dumb, dumb, dumb. I would have said to Moses, "Intervene right now. I'm sick of frogs, and I can't stand them for one more minute. Do it now!" But not Pharaoh. He said, "Do it tomorrow."

One of my favorite quotations is from Billy Sunday, who said, "A sinner can repent but stupid is forever." Sometimes the explanation for a broken rope is simply that you did something dumb. If I don't prepare for my sermon on Sunday and say something like, "I'll trust the Holy Spirit," I may bore the people, mishandle God's

Word, and turn off the unbelievers, who may have dropped in on the service. Suppose, after the service is over, I go to my wife and say, "Honey, that was a real bomb this morning. I'll just have to believe that God is teaching me something. I wish I knew what it is."

I have an extremely honest wife, and if I should say that to her, she would say to me, "Steve, the only thing God is trying to teach you is that you are lazy. He is saying to you that it is dumb to try to teach His Word without preparation." Sometimes broken ropes result from our own stupidity.

The Natural Consequences

Thirdly, some broken ropes occur because that's the way the world works. One of the saddest passages in the entire Bible is what followed after David, the friend of God, had committed adultery with Bathsheba and caused the death of her husband, Uriah. Bathsheba was pregnant with David's child. The prophet Nathan confronted David with his sin.

> Then David said to Nathan, "I have sinned against the LORD." And Nathan said to David, "The LORD also has put away your sin; you shall not die. However, because by this deed you have given great occasion to the enemies of the LORD to blaspheme, the child also who is born to you shall surely die."
>
> 2 Sam. 12:13–14

A lot of people believe that God created laws to keep us from having any fun. Not so. God has given us laws to warn us of danger. The Jews purposefully consider Holy Torah as God's greatest gift. It is through the law that we know God's will. If we ignore God's laws, we do so at our own peril.

We are now plagued (and I use the word carefully) with some very frightening sexually transmitted diseases. There are those who would say that God looks down from heaven and says, "Ah, ha. I caught you, and now you're going to get it." Then He gives AIDS or herpes to those who have done immoral things. That's not true. But the fact remains that if we had obeyed God's laws from the beginning, we would not have problems with those diseases now. Those diseases are part of God's judgment, but not in the way some people think. They do not signify particular, angry, specific judgment on people who do wrong; rather they are the "built-in" consequences of ignoring God's clear directions.

The Cross represents the place where Christ died for our sins and is the sign of God's love. But it is also the sign of God's hurt. Every time someone dies of AIDS, I believe God weeps just as a mother weeps when her child—the one she told to stay in the yard—climbs over a fence and gets hit by a car.

God has given us His Word, which shows us the best way to live. If we refuse to live that way, we can still find forgiveness because of the Cross. But sometimes the consequences of our refusal to follow God's map brings terrible tragedy.

This is an old story, but a good one. A little boy was angry and rebellious. His father (who probably had never read a book of child psychology) called him out to the back of the house and said, "Son, every time you disobey me, I am going to drive a nail into this post."

As time passed, the boy noticed that the post was filling up with nails. Finally, seeing what was happening, he went to his father and said, "Father, I never realized before how often I disobey you. Will you forgive me?"

"Of course, I'll forgive you," the father answered and he proceeded to pull every one of the nails out of the post. "Now, Son, all the nails are gone." The father noticed that his son was crying and asked him why.

"The nails are gone," the boy said through his sobs, "but the scars are still there."

You Don't Deserve Broken Ropes Because of Your Sin

Sometimes when our ropes break God is allowing us to face the natural consequences of our sin. But there is no direct, absolute correlation between breaking ropes and our breaking God's laws. In fact, I believe that most of the bad things that happen to us do not happen to us because of our wrongdoing.

Charles Colson recently wrote about his experience of cancer surgery in a *Christianity Today* article. Listen to his testimony:

> My suffering provided some fresh insights as well into the health and wealth gospel. If God really delivers His people from all pain and illness, as is so often claimed, why was I so sick? Had my faith become weak? Had I fallen from favor?
>
> No, I had always recognized such teaching as false theology. But after four weeks in a maximum-care unit, I came to see it as something else: a presumptuous stumbling block to real evangelism.
>
> During my nightly walks through the hospital corridors, dragging an IV pole behind me, I often met an Indian man whose two-year-old son had had two failed

kidney transplants, a brain aneurysm, and was now blind for life.

When the father, a Hindu, discovered I was a Christian, he asked if God would heal his son if he, too, was born again. He said he had heard things like that on television.

As I listened, I realized how arrogant health and wealth religion sounds to suffering families: Christians can all be spared suffering, but little Hindu children go blind. One couldn't blame a Hindu or Muslim or agnostic for resenting, even hating, such a God.

I told my Hindu friend about Jesus. Yes, he may miraculously intervene in our lives. But we come to God not because of what He may do to spare us suffering, but because Christ is truth. What He does promise us is much more—the forgiveness of sin and eternal life. I left the hospital with my friend studying Christian literature, the Bible, and my own account in *Born Again*. If he becomes a Christian, it won't be on false pretenses.[1]

Chuck had done nothing to deserve cancer. Of course, Chuck is a sinner. But his cancer can't be correlated to anything he has done wrong. Perhaps the only reason Chuck had to suffer cancer was so he could meet that Hindu man.

Now, I want you to think about your broken ropes. If you are human, you have probably been trying to confess your sins to God, hoping that once you are forgiven your rope won't be broken anymore. If your rope is still broken after you have confessed and promised God that you won't do anything bad ever again, you probably feel even more guilty than you did before. It can be a vicious circle. Before you start going around and around, let me tell you some things you ought to know.

You Deserve a Lot Worse

If you got what you really deserved, you would be dead now. People are always saying that they hope God is a just God. If He is just, we are all in trouble. The Bible teaches that we are sinners and that there is not one good person in the world:

> *There is none righteous, no, not one;*
> *There is none who understands;*
> *There is none who seeks after God.*
> *They have all gone out of the way;*
> *They have together become unprofitable;*
> *There is none who does good, no, not one.*
> *Rom. 3:10–12*

A policeman stopped me the other day, and I had done nothing wrong. I live on an island, and in order to get to the island without paying a toll, one has to have a special license plate. My plate had become bent and didn't look proper, so the policeman followed me for about two miles, turned on his red blinking light, and pulled me over. My first reaction when I noticed him in the rearview mirror was indignation: "I am not speeding; I am properly licensed; I have run no stop signs; I have made no wrong turns; I have not gone the wrong way down a one-way street! How dare he follow me as if I were a common criminal!"

But before he turned on his light, my head had cleared and I thought of all the times I had broken the law. I wasn't speeding then, but I have, on occasion, gone over the speed limit. I was properly licensed, but when I first came to Florida I had the wrong license for more than two months. I had not run a stop sign then, but I had before on a number of occasions. I had made no wrong turns or gone the wrong way down a one-way street—that morning. By the time he pulled me over, I had decided that if he threw me in jail and threw away the key, I would be receiving the just deserts of my driving record in the past.

Before you are too quick to judge (especially my friends who will take great delight in the above confession) let me ask you a couple of questions: Don't you watch out for policemen on the highway, even when you have done nothing wrong? When you see a police officer driving behind you, don't you slow down, even if you were driving under the speed limit? Of course you do! Do you know why? Because you are just as guilty as I am. Maybe you did nothing wrong right then, but you did wrong sometime. If you got what you really deserved, given all the times you have broken the traffic laws and weren't caught, where would you be right now?

Life is like that too. Think for a moment of all the bad things you have done in your life. What if God tried to balance the books right now? Where would you be? You would be holding so many broken ropes that you'd have to carry them off in a truck.

What's the point? The hurt you experience is not related to your sin. If it were, you would hurt a whole lot more.

Bad People Do Prosper

Your broken rope might logically have something to do with your sin, but then the converse would also have to be true; that is, turkeys do quite well sometimes, thank you. If God did correlate our sin with a broken rope and our goodness with a holding rope, how come so many bad people do so well?

The psalmist had some questions about why the wicked prosper:

> *For the wicked boasts of his heart's desire;*
> *He blesses the greedy and renounces the LORD.*
> *The wicked in his proud countenance does not seek God;*
> *God is in none of his thoughts.*
> *His ways are always prospering.*
>
> Ps. 10:3–5a

It would be nice if every time we were good we were rewarded for being good and every time we were bad we were punished for being bad. If that were true, everybody would be good and nobody would be bad. But it simply doesn't work that way. Someday when God balances the books, just rewards will be given, but only a fool would say that it works that way right now. Of course, there is a long-term reward for righteousness, and there is a long-term liability for evil. But in the short haul, the consequences are sometimes quite different.

One of the problems with prosperity theology is that it makes promises we have no right to make to people. If you are a Christian for what you can get out of it, then you aren't going to get much out of it. If you are obedient because of the rewards you will receive, then your rewards are going to be very small. If you are kind because kindness pays, then you are probably going to the poorhouse. If your faith is exercised only on your behalf, then your faith is selfish and will probably die.

I have a friend named Cleve Bell, who works in a prison ministry. I love to go to the prison with him just to watch him work. He never preaches. He dialogues. One time an old man and a young man were in a small group in the chapel where he was speaking. The young man got up and testified that he had become a Christian, and Cleve affirmed him in his decision. Then the old man got up and said that he had been serving the Lord for almost two years.

"I noticed," Cleve said, rather harshly I thought, "that you are up for parole next week. What are you going to do if they don't let you out?"

"It will be O.K.," the man said. "I can serve Christ wherever I am. If He chooses to leave me here, I will serve Him here."

"You have to do more than that!" Cleve said.

"What else do I have to do?"

"You have to repent of the example you gave to some of these young men in this place. Every time they looked at you, you had a chick on your arm, gold on your wrist, and you were driving a big, expensive car. There are a lot of people who are in jail or on drugs right now because of the example you gave them before you were put in prison.

Then that old man did something I'll never forget. He walked up to the young man who had just become a Christian and said, "Son, I want to ask your forgiveness for giving you the wrong model. You needed someone who would tell you the truth. I lied to you by letting you see my money, my women, and my cars. I'm sorry."

Cleve just beamed. He hugged that old man, and we all rejoiced in the obvious reality of his commitment to Christ.

But, as a matter of fact, that man is a good example

of the point I am making. In spite of his sin, he had had everything he wanted. I love the comment of Willie Sutton, who was asked why he robbed banks. "Because," he said, "that's where the money is."

If there were no money in robbing banks, nobody would rob them. If drug pushers didn't do well, nobody would push drugs. If sin had no payback, nobody would ever sin. But we all know that it does.

If you think your broken rope has to do with your sin, you ought to look around. You might do better by sinning more. Sometimes the wicked do prosper.

You Are Forgiven

There is one other thing to think about if you believe you're hurting because you've done something wrong: forgiveness. Do you believe that God forgives us? The Bible says, "If we confess our sins, He is faithful and just to forgive us our sins and to cleanse us from all unrighteousness" (1 John 1:9). If God were still exacting a price for your sin (i.e., correlating your sin with your broken rope), then the cross of Christ was a farce and you aren't forgiven until you "work it off."

I had a friend who was unfaithful to his wife more than twenty years ago. He came to me saying that everything bad that had ever happened to him had happened because of his unfaithfulness. When I asked him if he had confessed it before God, he answered that not a day had gone by in the last twenty years that he had not confessed his sin. After we talked about it, we decided that he ought to confess it to his wife.

It was difficult to go to her after all those years. In some cases it is not necessary or helpful to confess adultery to one's spouse. The confession can destroy the spouse and hurt the marriage even more than it has already been hurt. But in this case (I knew his wife), it was needed. We prayed about it, and he left the office in fear and trembling but knowing what he had to do.

I saw him a week later, and he was on top of the world. He was a new man. I asked him how his wife had responded and he said, "She told me that she had known from the beginning and was just waiting for me to tell her—if I wanted to."

"How do you feel now?" I asked.

"I feel free. For the first time in twenty years I feel free."

A year later this man experienced some great financial reverses. He lost his job and his home. He then had to face major surgery. When I visited him in the hospital, he said to me, "You know, Pastor, if I had not confessed what happened twenty years ago I would believe that all this happened to punish me. I don't think I could stand that."

Maybe you don't know for sure that you're forgiven. If you don't, please take my word for it. If you have confessed your sin, you really are forgiven. God doesn't have a perverse desire to exact a price from you greater than the price that was paid on the cross. That was enough.

Are you old enough to remember the blackout of the sixties? Almost the entire northeastern part of the United States lost its power. People were stuck in elevators; television and radio stations had to go on emergency power; there were no street lights; and hospitals had to cut back on all except emergency surgery. It was a very frightening experience. As I remember, the whole thing happened because of a series of problems at a number of power companies. None of the problems was particularly great, but together, they created a massive loss of power.

A friend tells the story of a little boy who, during the blackout, was acting very guilty. When his parents asked him what was wrong, he broke down and cried. Through his sobs he confessed that on the way home from school he had kicked a power pole.

There is something about that story which is not only sad but also arrogant. The little boy assumed responsibility for an error far greater than he could ever have caused. When bad things happen to us we are sometimes like that little boy. We blame ourselves for tragedies beyond our control, that we never could have purposed. We figure that a loving, kind, and compassionate God has changed everything including His nature to "get us" and make us pay for our sin.

He hasn't!

If He has, we have a greater problem than guilt.

7

Where Did They Go Wrong?

In the last chapter we saw that there is no direct, absolute correlation between your breaking ropes and your breaking God's law. That is an important truth for you to remember. Let me give you another one: There is no direct, absolute correlation between other people's breaking ropes and *their* breaking God's law.

As they were walking, Jesus and His disciples saw a man who had been blind from birth. "And His disciples asked Him, saying, 'Rabbi, who sinned, this man or his parents, that he was born blind?' Jesus answered, 'Neither this man nor his parents sinned, but that the works of God should be revealed in him'" (John 9:2–3).

Learning a New Way to Relate

Over the years I have often ministered to people who were suffering from cancer. The word *cancer* solicits interesting responses. Dr. David Seel, a medical missionary to Korea who deals primarily with cancer, made an interesting observation about the similarities between cancer and Satan himself, "A cancer surgeon worthy of the term will develop a belligerent sense of outrage toward his enemy. Cancer has indeed come to signify to me the embodiment of evil, a prototype of Satan."[1]

His observation does not differ greatly from most of our observations. We would rather deal with anything other than cancer. Just the use of the term the big "C," rouses in us feelings of dread and anxiety.

It is interesting to note how people deal with the information that they have cancer. But it is far more interesting to see how people deal with someone else's cancer. In the early stages the friends of the cancer victim give support and encouragement. But as the cancer develops, the friends start disappearing. They visit less often, and they avoid any discussion of the disease. There is an almost neurotic avoidance of the word *cancer*.

If the victim is terminal, he or she is often forced to deal with its harsh realities alone. Friends stop coming by altogether. Doctors and nurses even find excuses not to visit the patient's room. Of course, in most cases, the family doesn't leave, but even the family tries to ignore the reality of death. One man told me, "Pastor, I feel like I'm not here. Nobody will talk to me. It seems that my friends have dropped me. Don't they know it isn't catching?"

The way most people deal with another's cancer is symbolic of the way most people deal with any tragedy in another's life. Christians must learn to relate to one another in tragedy as well as good times. God has given us to each other.

For as the body is one and has many members, but all the members of that one body, being many, are one body, so also is Christ. For by one Spirit we were all baptized into one body—whether Jews or Greeks, whether slaves or free—and have all been made to drink into one Spirit. . . . And if one member suffers, all the members suffer with it; or if one member is honored,all the members rejoice with it. Now you are the body of Christ, and members individually.

1 Cor. 12:12–13; 26–27

What Job's Friends Did Right

We can observe Job and his friends to learn better ways to help each other. Job suffered but not because he had done anything wrong. His godliness and integrity made accusation almost impossible. But notice the way Job's friends related to him.

Be There

First, they were there. They didn't say everything right; they missed the point, and they were sometimes harsh. But they were there: "Now when Job's three friends heard of all this adversity that had come upon him, each one came from his own place—Eliphaz the Temanite, Bildad the Shuhite, and Zophar the Naamathite. For they had made an appointment together to come and mourn with him, and to comfort him" (Job 2:11).

I remember the first time I had to deal with a death in my congregation. I knew all the right things to say; I had been trained in dealing with grief; I was reasonably articulate. I prepared what I would say to the grieving wife, and as I drove to her house, I went over it in my mind.

But when I got there, I lost it all. I tried to say some comforting things and made such a mess out of it that I just shut up and sat on the couch. It was one of the most miserable times in my ministry. When I drove away from the house, I was ashamed and humiliated. I was a pastor of a flock, yet this pastor had done nothing except to sit and watch.

After the funeral two or three days later, the widow came into my study. I started to apologize to her, but before I could speak she said, "Pastor, I want to thank you for all you have done for me. I don't know how I could have gotten through this without you."

I couldn't believe my ears. "But," I said, "I didn't do anything."

I'll never forget that woman's statement. She smiled and said, "You were there."

Never underestimate the value of being there. Too often, when our friends are going through tough times, we do everything in our power to avoid them. Perhaps we think their tragedy will be contagious. Maybe we don't know what to say. It could be that our being with people who are hurting reminds us of our own vulnerability. Whatever the reason, avoidance is wrong. *Be there.*

I love the old sermon illustration about the two buddies who fought together during World War II. They had grown up together, they had joined the army together, and they had served together. During a battle one of the young men was shot and was dying in no man's land. His cries could be heard in the trenches, and his friend went to the sergeant and asked if he could go out to his buddy. The sergeant refused, saying, "Son, I know you two were close, but I don't want to lose two of you. Your buddy is going to die. There is no use for you to die too."

The young man persisted, however, and finally the sergeant, against his better judgment, allowed the young man to retrieve his buddy. An hour later the young man came climbing back into the trenches carrying the body of his buddy. The wounded soldier was obviously dead.

"I told you you shouldn't have gone," the sergeant said. "He's dead and it wasn't worth it."

"Oh, yes, it was worth it," the dead soldier's friend replied. "When I got to him he was still alive. He said to me as I knelt down beside him, 'Jim, I knew you would come.' It was worth it."

Keep Quiet

Second, Job's friends were not only there but they were also quiet, at least at first: "So they sat down with him on the ground seven days and seven nights, and no one spoke a word to him, for they saw that his grief was very great" (Job 2:13).

Often people who want to help someone going through a difficult time will come to me and say something like, "Pastor, I want to help him or her but I don't know what to say." On those occasions I generally feel relieved, because not knowing what to say in the presence of a friend's suffering is a tremendous asset. If you don't know what to say, then don't say anything.

If you've ever suffered, you've found that those who talked the most usually helped the least. Job's friends had enough sense, in the beginning, anyway, not to say anything.

When my brother died, a number of close friends, without my knowledge, flew to North Carolina and attended the funeral. They hardly spoke a word. They simply cried with our family and let us know that they were suffering too. Not once did they give me any clichés or pious platitudes. They didn't tell me theological truths I already knew or try to explain why God allows such tragedy. They were there and they were quiet. The memory of their silent, loving support will minister to me for the rest of my life.

When people are suffering don't blabber. You don't know why they are suffering any more than they do. Just be there and be silent. It can make a big difference.

Don't Gossip

Third, when Job's rope broke, his friends didn't talk behind his back. Throughout the book his friends said some pretty harsh things. Job was "ticked" at them, and he had every right to be. But the positive thing was that they didn't talk behind his back. What they said, they said to his face (not that they should have done that).

My pastor friend replaced a pastor who was retiring after having served some twenty-five years in a church. My friend was not very popular with his new congregation. After having served the church for almost a year, his wife delivered a stillborn baby. The general consensus of the congregation was that the baby was stillborn because my friend was out of the will of God. By the time that spurious opinion got back to my friend, it was told him as if from the mouth of God. My friend was devastated.

When our friends are suffering we fear that the same thing will happen to us. In an attempt to comfort each other, we often issue lines like, "Sam never was very committed. God is chastening him." Everybody agrees and then everybody feels better. "Sarah was a flirt, and it always hurt her husband. Now God is balancing the books." Everybody agrees and then everybody feels better. "It is a tragedy, but Bill asked for it in the way he was living. If he had only heeded God's Word then this never would have happened." Everybody agrees and then everybody feels better.

Give Your Friend Freedom

Job's friends did another thing right. They allowed him to express his bitterness and anger. You will find

some of the most bitter words you've ever heard coming
from Job's mouth:

"May the day perish on which I was born,
And the night in which it was said,
'A male child is conceived.'
. . . .
Because it did not shut up the doors of my mother's womb,
Nor hide sorrow from my eyes.
Why did I not die at birth?
Why did I not perish when I came from the womb?"

Job 3:3, 10–11

It takes a lot of strength and love to listen to that
kind of emotion pouring out of a friend. Most folks
would have left, but Job's friends didn't. They stayed
and listened. As I've mentioned previously, there is a
ministry of listening to bitterness. It is important when
you are trying to meet the needs of someone whose rope
has broken.

I got a letter the other day from a young man who
paid me a very high compliment. His father had died
over a year ago, but during the process, he had been his
father's primary emotional and physical support. Every-
time I met with him after his dad's funeral, he expressed
a variety of problems. It happened so often that I sus-
pected something was bothering him other than the
problems he voiced. One day I asked him, "Jim, have
you buried your father yet?"

The explosion which came from him surprised me.
"That's a horrible thing to say," he shouted. "I loved my
father, and I miss him very much. Of course, I've buried
him."

He paused, and I decided to follow the string as far

as it would go. In the silence I asked, "Jim, why are you so angry at me for asking you that question? Are you angry at me, or are you angry at your father? Better yet, are you angry at God?"

The last thing I expected was tears, but that is exactly what happened. He began to weep.

"You know, Jim, you seem to have suppressed a lot of your anger. You need to get that out in the sunshine where it will die. If you want me, I'll be here as your sounding board. Just call me."

The next day he called me and said that he had decided to take me up on my offer.

A couple of days later he came in, and for two hours he poured out his anger and bitterness. Once the trickle began, it got stronger and stronger until it was a flood. His language was coarse, and his words were stinging.

My friend was angry at God for having put him through all of the hurt. He was angry at his father for dying. He was angry at his friends for not caring. He was mad at his religion for not giving him the answers he needed. He was angry at his mother for leaving them. He was angry at his grandmother for telling his mother to leave. On and on it went.

To be perfectly honest, it was difficult to sit there and listen. I wanted to defend God, but I figured I would just be still and let God defend Himself. I wanted to defend his friends, because I knew some of them and I knew they weren't as uncaring as he said. But I figured that if those friends needed to be defended they could do it themselves. I wanted to defend his parents, his mother, his past. But, with great effort, I kept quiet. When he was finished, he felt spent and I felt dirty.

About a week ago I go a letter from him. When I

saw the return address, I wanted to throw it away. But I opened it, and I found myself reading the words of a different person: *"Steve, your willingness to sit there and listen to all that dirt has changed my life. I feel a great burden has been lifted, and I haven't felt this good in years. When I think of all the things I said to you, I feel a bit uncomfortable, but the good thing is that I know you understand."*

Not everyone can listen to bitterness, and I don't want to do it often. But when people find their ropes broken, they aren't rational or clear or loving. Somebody has to allow them to ventilate their hostility. Somebody has got to lance the boil. Job's friends did that for him, and even though he didn't understand, it was a great gift.

What Job's Friends Did Wrong

Job's friends also did a lot that was wrong. We can learn from their negative example too.

Don't Be Intellectual

First, they tried to have an intellectual discussion with Job while he was holding his broken rope in his hand.

> *Then Eliphaz the Temanite answered and said:*
>
> *"If one attempts a word with you, will you become weary?*
> *But who can withhold himself from speaking?*
> *Surely you have instructed many,*
> *And you have strengthened weak hands.*
> *Your words have upheld him who was stumbling,*
> *And you have strengthened the feeble knees;*
> *But now it comes upon you, and you are weary"*
>
> *Job 4:1–5a*

I heard the story of a chaplain in the Civil War. He was ministering to a group of Confederate soldiers pushing an army wagon out of a mud hole where it was stuck. The soldiers were wet and tired and up to their knees in mud. Standing next to one of the men, the chaplain asked, "Do you know Jesus as your Savior?"

Without looking up, the soldier replied, "This ain't no time for riddles, Reverend. I'm stuck in the mud."

When you are stuck in the mud it's not time to discuss the finer points of salvation. Similarly, when someone is suffering, it isn't the proper time to discuss the theological, philosophical, and metaphysial implications of the problem of suffering. Yet that is exactly what Job's friends did.

A friend's daughter died giving birth to her child. My friend was hurt and angry. He came storming into my study and practically yelled, "How could your God allow something like this to happen?" I asked him to sit down, and as soon as he did, he began to cry.

His tears flowed for a while, and then I said, "Ken, you need to know that God is the God of the mind as well as the God of the heart. We can talk about why these things happen sometime. But right now, you don't want those answers.

"You are hurt and angry, and what you need is someone who will accept your anger. I'm your man. When you're on the other side of this, we'll discuss some of those answers, but right now, let's pray."

During the next year my friend would see me and answer my question about how he was doing by saying, "I'm not doing too well, but I'm doing better. But don't forget, Steve, you promised to talk to me about the reason for suffering when I got well."

117

After the year was over, my friend didn't bring up his need for intellectual answers to the problem of suffering. I asked him not too long ago if he was ready to have that discussion. "No, Steve," he said, "I don't need the answers. I probably wouldn't understand them anyway. I'm just a simple man, and I've decided to trust God, even if I don't understand."

When someone's rope has broken and their hurt is terrible, for their sake, don't engage in intellectual discussions about the nature of breaking ropes.

You Aren't Beyond Reproach

Second, Job's friends took a superior position. After all, they thought, Job's rope had broken and that meant that he had done something wrong. Their ropes had not broken, thus it followed logically that they had not done the bad things Job had done. Listen to Eliphaz's superior, arrogant condemnation of Job:

> *"Call out now;*
> *Is there anyone who will answer you?*
> *And to which of the holy ones will you turn?*
> *For wrath kills a foolish man,*
> *And envy slays a simply one.*
> . . . .
>
> *But as for me, I would seek God,*
> *And to God I would commit my cause—*
> . . . .
> *Behold, happy is the man whom God corrects."*
>
> *Job 5:1–2, 8, 17*

Job felt the sting and responded:

"No doubt you are the people,
And wisdom will die with you!
But I have understanding as well as you;
I am not inferior to you."
                                        Job 12:1–3a

Kent Keller, the singles minister at the church I serve, gave me a personal ad he had found in a singles magazine. It read: "Outworlder. No home to phone. Male Human, 25, Quasimodo looks, dull, insecure, humorless, likes pop tarts, legos. Seeks female counterpart to share empty, meaningless existence. Send police composite. No. F–150." Kent said he would expect the person who wrote that to get hundreds of inquiries. I suspect Kent's right. Whatever else that young man is, he won't be judgmental about anybody else's condition. And people are looking for other people who will accept them.

Preachers and teachers in the church today often give the impression that they've achieved all that they preach or teach. The congregation or class then thinks, *The Christian faith is only for good people, and I am not a good person, so the Christian faith isn't for me.* That kind of preaching and teaching, combined with dishonesty about personal tragedy and hurt, implies that the Christian faith is only for good people who are doing quite well.

Conclusion: The Christian faith is not for me.

I have a friend from Pittsburgh who once told me, "Steve, for twenty years I have been listening to preachers say they were sinners. You are the first one I have ever believed." That, believe it or not, was a high

119

compliment. None of us can say as an outsider what we think of the human race. This is a bad world and we are sinners. No one can speak from the pinnacle of purity. It is important that we identify with those to whom God has sent us. If we can't identify with them, we ought to stay away from them.

I love Emily Dickinson's untitled poem from her collected works:

> *I'm nobody! Who are you?*
> *Are you nobody, too?*
> *Then there's a pair of us—don't tell!*
> *They'd banish us, you know.*
>
> *How dreary to be somebody!*
> *How public, like a frog,*
> *To tell your name the livelong day*
> *To an admiring bog!*[2]

There are no super-Christians. Jesus died for us because we are sinners. When we approach someone who has just felt the snap of a broken rope, we had better take the position of one who, if we got what we deserved, would be holding a frazzled, broken rope too.

You Can't Speak for God

Third, the friends of Job presumed to speak for God. Zophar made some interesting comments to Job in their first cycle of debate:

> *"Can you search out the deep things of God?*
> *Can you find out the limits of the Almighty?*
> . . . .

If He passes by, imprisons, and gathers to judgment,
Then who can hinder Him?
For He knows deceitful men;
He sees wickedness also.
. . . .
If iniquity were in your hand, and you put it far away,
And would not let wickedness dwell in your tents;
Then surely you could lift up your face without spot;
Yes, you could be steadfast, and not fear."
Job 11:7, 10–11, 14–15

Very interesting. Zophar said that one couldn't explain God, but then he went about trying to explain Him. Presuming to speak for God on almost any issue is very dangerous.

A wonderful couple in my church gave birth to a baby boy born with some very serious medical problems. Not too long ago Matthew (the baby) had to go through a life-threatening procedure, the most serious of a number of surgical procedures he had already undergone. Our congregation was deeply affected by Matthew, and we prayed a lot during his surgery. We had faith and concern. We trusted Jesus.

Do you know what happened? Matthew died. Matthew's parents and our congregation were devastated.

During Matthew's illness a great number of people brought "messages from the Lord." Some said, "The Lord has revealed to me that Matthew is going to be fine." Others said, "Matthew is going to die, but God said that He was in charge and for you not to worry." "I have been speaking to the Lord about Matthew, and it has been revealed to me that, while he will go through a difficult time, he will be completely healed."

Now I don't question the motivation of those people who felt deeply for Matthew and his parents. However, when Matthew died, a lot of "messengers" were strangely silent. If God is teaching a lesson or has a message, that's His business and He is perfectly capable of communicating with the sufferer. We don't need to speak for God.

You Aren't Immune to Suffering

Fourth, Job's friends assumed that what was happening to Job couldn't happen to them. In the second cycle of debates, Eliphaz the Temanite told Job that "the wicked man writhes with pain all his days, / And the number of years is hidden from the oppressor" (Job 15:20). Now you need to know that what Eliphaz was saying to Job is less important than what he was saying about himself—that is, if bad people suffer, then good people don't. I'm not suffering; therefore, I must be good. Further, Eliphaz was suggesting that because he was good, he wouldn't ever have to suffer the way Job was. Don't bet on it, Eliphaz!

Whenever our Christian brothers or sisters suffer, we need to realize that the same thing that is happening to them today could happen to us tomorrow. We must be careful of the words we dish out now. We may have to eat them later.

Don't Be Impractical

Finally, Job's friends didn't do anything practical. They just talked. Job needed someone to bind up his wounds. He needed money; maybe he even needed a hug. All he got from his friends was words.

The story is told of a little boy who was sent to the

grocery store to buy milk. On his way home he dropped the milk bottle and it broke, splashing glass and milk all over the street. The little boy began to wail, attracting a crowd of people. One man told the boy that his mother would understand. Another person said that it was no use to cry over spilt milk. But one woman said to the child, "Son, I care that you have spilt your milk." Then she turned to the crowd and said, "I care a quarter's worth. How much do you care?"

Doing something practical is often just what is needed when you have a friend whose rope is broken.

C. S. Lewis is one of my few heroes. After his death, it was discovered that he had carried on extensive correspondence with people all over the world. In the introduction to *Letters to an American Lady*, a book of Lewis's letters, the editor Clyde Kilby said about the woman Lewis was writing, "Once financially independent, she had fallen upon privation and, what was worse, serious family problems. In due course Lewis arranged through his American publishers a small stipend for her, and this continues to the present."[3]

When I found out what Lewis had done financially for this lady whom he had never met, the words he wrote in his letters to her carried far greater weight. Sometimes when our friend's rope has broken, our friend simply needs someone who can meet a few practical needs, someone who knows how to tie knots.

Christians ought to know how to tie knots.

8

The Demon of Discouragement

Charles Spurgeon often dealt with the problem of discouragement. He told his students: "One crushing stroke has sometimes laid the minister very low. The brother most relied upon becomes a traitor. Judas lifts up his heel against the man who trusted him, and the preacher's heart for the moment fails him. . . . Strife, also, and division, and slander, and foolish censures, have often laid holy men prostrate, and made them go 'as with a sword in their bones.' Hard words wound some delicate minds very keenly. . . . By experience the soul is hardened to the rough blows which are inevitable in our warfare; but at first these things utterly stagger us, and send us to our homes wrapped in a horror of great darkness. . . .

"When troubles multiply, and discouragements follow each other in long succession, like Job's messengers, then, too, amid the perturbation of soul occasioned by evil tidings, despondency despoils the heart of all its peace. Constant dropping wears away stones, and the bravest minds feel the fret of repeated afflictions. If a scanty cupboard is rendered a severer trial by the sickness of a wife or the loss of a child, and if ungenerous remarks of hearers are followed by the opposition of deacons and the coolness of members, then, like Jacob, we are apt to cry, 'All these things are against me.'. . . Accumulated distresses increase each other's weight; they play into each other's hands, and like bands of robbers, ruthlessly destroy our comfort Wave upon wave is severe work for the strongest swimmer. The place where two seas meet strains the most seaworthy keel. If there were regulated pause between the buffetings of adversity, the spirit would stand prepared; but when they come suddenly and heavily, like the battering of great hailstones, the pilgrim may well be amazed. The last ounce is laid upon us, what wonder if we for awhile are ready to give up the ghost!"[1]

Spurgeon, of course, was talking to ministers, but everyone can identify with his comments. One of the great problems with broken ropes is the inevitable discouragement which follows. How does one deal with the demon of discouragement? Let's talk about it.

The Great Cloud of Witnesses

One of the keys to dealing with discouragement is found in Hebrews 12:1-3:

> *Therefore we also, since we are surrounded by so great a cloud of witnesses, let us lay aside every weight, and the sin which so easily ensnares us, and let us run with endurance the race that is set before us, looking unto Jesus, the author and finisher of our faith, who for the joy that was set before Him endured the cross, despising the shame, and has sat down at the right hand of the throne of God. For consider Him who endured such hostility from sinners against Himself, lest you become weary and discouraged in your souls.*

The writer of Hebrews first suggests that we are sur-

125

rounded by witnesses. The eleventh chapter of Hebrews lists a number of Old Testament characters who endured great suffering and who persevered through faith. Talk about broken ropes! The writer ends that chapter talking about people of God who were mocked and beaten, who were stoned, imprisoned, sawn in half, and who had no homes (see Heb. 11:36–39).

The twelfth chapter of Hebrews opens by saying that we are surrounded by a cloud of witnesses; that is, "You are not by yourself. If your rope has broken, look at the broken ropes of others who have gone on to successfully complete their race. Be encouraged by them."

The apostle Paul wrote the Christians in Corinth about the trials he and his friends had experienced—trials so great that they "despaired even of life" (2 Cor. 1:8). I wouldn't wish that kind of hurt on anyone, but I'm glad Paul went through it. It makes me feel better about my own discouragement.

Discouragement, you see, is almost always marked by a feeling of aloneness. You feel that no one could possibly understand, no one could possibly have had the kind of troubles you have, no one could possibly be as discouraged as you are at the moment. It helps sometimes to remember that others have indeed shared the occasion of suffering.

An old spiritual says, "When I've done the best I can and my friends misunderstand, / Thou Who knowest all about me, stand by me." But, you see, all of your friends don't misunderstand. You just think they do. Discouragement is a part of living.

In the early part of the sixteenth century a man by the name of Thomas Bilney became convinced of the need for the Bible in the lives of believers. Because he was vocal about those convictions, he was burned at the stake in Norwich, England, in 1531. His story is not uncommon. Many people have burned at the stake because of their convictions.

Standing in the crowd on the day Bilney was executed was a young man named Hugh Latimer. A graduate of Cambridge, Latimer was so influenced by the life and death of Bilney that he committed his life to the propagation of Bilney's faith. Later, Latimer became a bishop of the church. When "Bloody" Mary came to the throne, Hugh Latimer was among those who were tortured and killed. While he was burning at the stake, he turned to a fellow bishop and friend being executed with him and said, "Be of good comfort, Master Ridley. We shall this day light such a candle by God's grace in England as, I trust, shall never be put out."

I think of Bilney and Latimer when I get discouraged. They are a few of the witnesses who minister to me when my rope has broken. I have also asked God to give me enough grace to "keep on trucking" so that I may be a witness to others whose rope has broken.

The Demon of Guilt

The passage quoted from Hebrews 12 not only suggests that we have company, but also reminds us that we have been forgiven. The writer says, "Let us lay aside every weight, and the sin which so easily ensnares us." I don't know about you, but when I'm discouraged, the first thing I do is evaluate my sin—and I find a whole lot. Guilt, you see, is part of the demonic element in discouragement.

How do you lay aside the weight and sin? You do it with confession, resting in the promise that "if we confess our sins, He is faithful and just to forgive us our sins and to cleanse us from all unrighteousness" (1 John 1:9). Discouragement hardly ever grows in the soil of forgiveness.

When I was in high school, a group of my friends and I had an all-night party. About three in the morning someone suggested that we go swimming in the pool of an exclusive club and hotel in town. It was very dark when we climbed the fence and approached the pool. We were having a good time until one of my friends jumped off the high diving board, sitting on an inner tube. When he hit the water, it sounded like a shotgun blast. Before we knew what was happening the lights started going on in the hotel, and the night watchman came out of his office with his gun and a flashlight. We ran.

As I was climbing over the fence and running to the car, I looked back over my shoulder to see my friend—the one who had jumped off the high diving board—trying to climb the fence holding on to the inner tube. "Bill," I yelled back, "drop the inner tube or the sucker's going to get you!"

Guilt is like that inner tube. If your rope has broken, you already have enough trouble without adding guilt to the pile. You've already seen that there is no absolute correlation between your sin and your broken ropes. So, don't forget to throw away the inner tube. Examine your life, accept your forgiveness, and don't keep carrying around the inner tube of guilt.

Power to Endure

The author of Hebrews says that we are empowered to endure our broken ropes by "looking unto Jesus, the author and finisher of our faith, who for the joy that was set before Him endured the cross, despising the shame, and has sat down at the right hand of the throne of God" (Heb.12:2).

Hopelessness is the twin sister of discouragement. No Christian need ever feel hopeless, because we have the choice of looking to Jesus rather than at our circumstances.

Do you remember when Jesus told Peter to walk on the waves? At first the disciples thought Jesus was a ghost, but Jesus quickly told them who He was and settled their fears. Peter, evidently, still had some doubt that Jesus was who He said He was, so he made a simple request:

"Lord, if it is You, command me to come to You on the water." So He said, "Come." And when Peter had come down out of the boat, he walked on the water to go to Jesus. But when he saw that the wind was boisterous, he was afraid; and beginning to sink he cried out, saying, "Lord, save me!" And immediately Jesus stretched out His hand and caught him, and said to him, "O you of little faith, why did you doubt?" And when they got into the boat, the wind ceased.

Matt. 14:28–32

Peter's problem was that he began to look at the waves instead of at Jesus. I don't know about you, but if the waves had been big, I would have looked at them too. When waves are big, the danger is real, and we think about them to the exclusion of anything else. Some broken ropes are so devastating, it's hard to look at anything except the broken rope. When you're going through a divorce, when you have cancer, when you're

129

losing your children, others may easily say look at Jesus, but it's very hard to do.

All of that granted, there is still a difference when Jesus is with us. Looking to Jesus may not be easy, and we can't ignore the waves altogether. However, the point of Peter's experience was not to show that waves exist or how big they get but to show that Jesus was there. He was there for Peter, and He is there for us.

One of the many nice things about my wife, Anna, is that she always puts little notes in and around the clothes I pack when I leave home for a speaking engagement. Anna knows that I get nervous in academic settings (I ran away from kindergarten, and I struggled through the next twenty years of education) and that I have a great desire to do well and to have people like me and a great fear of failure. As I was dressing before a lecture I was to give at Denver Seminary, I found a note in my shoe: *"Just remember that nothing is going to happen today that Jesus can't handle."* That note reminded me about the One who owns me and for whom I speak. Because Anna helped me to focus on Jesus instead of myself and the situation, I felt a lot better.

"But you don't understand," you are saying. "My broken rope is a lot more than a little fear about speaking in a seminary. I am really going through a very difficult time. I'm so discouraged that I don't think I can go on."

Let me tell you something: The principle is the same no matter what the circumstances. Either Jesus is there or He isn't. Either Jesus does have something to do with your situation or He doesn't. If He doesn't, you have a whole lot bigger problem than discouragement. But the Scripture is clear about His involvement: "And we know that all things work together for good to those who love

God, to those who are the called according to His purpose" (Rom. 8:28). Focus on Him. It can make a big difference.

In the closing pages of this chapter I want to remind you of four important items we often forget when we're discouraged.

1. Remember the Past

First, don't forget the past. The past is the informer of the present. Not everything said by Job's friends was wrong. A case in point is Bildad's first speech to Job:

"For inquire, please, of the former age,
And consider the things discovered by their fathers;
For we are but of yesterday, and know nothing,
Because our days on earth are a shadow.
Will they not teach you and tell you,
And utter words from their heart?"

Job 8:8–10

When you look at the history of God's people, you see God's faithfulness and love. When you look to your own past, you can also see God's faithfulness and love.

God has been building memorials in your life from the time you were born. What's a memorial? It's a memory of times when God has been faithful. If He was faithful in the past, He won't stop being faithful now or in the future.

If I had been standing on the side of the boat, watching Peter go under the waves, I would have shouted to him, "Hey Peter! You were walking. You were really walking on the water before you got so overwhelmed by the waves. You aren't going to drown. Jesus won't let you." If I could have gotten Peter's attention, maybe he would have climbed back up on the wave and ridden it to Jesus. Of course, he didn't. That's why Jesus reached down and pulled him out.

I'll bet Peter recorded in his memory those waves and Jesus' faithfulness on that day. I'll bet Peter thought about it the rest of his life.

I keep a diary. I must admit that I don't write in it very often. In fact, I don't write in it unless one of my ropes has broken. The diary records not my life but those places in my life when I was hurt and discouraged. When I think I've finally gotten into a hole from which I will never escape, I get out the diary and read about the other times when I thought I was in the same place. Then, I remember that I got out of the hole. It may have hurt, but by God's grace I got out of the hole. God always says to me on those occasions of diary reading, "Child, if I was faithful then, I will be faithful now."

2. Remember the Facts

Second, when you are discouraged, don't forget the facts. Paul instructed the people at Ephesus how to stand in the midst of a spiritual battle: "Therefore take up the whole armor of God, that you may be able to withstand in the evil day, and having done all, to stand. Stand therefore, having girded your waist with truth" (Eph. 6:13–14). Please note that Paul said we need to depend on truth for support; facts are the reality, not our feelings about the facts. One of the marks of discouragement is the "feeling" that God has gone away—that you aren't important and that you've been kidding yourself about your relationship with Him.

I heard the story of a man whose wife left him, children disowned him, and business failed. As he was walking down the street, he was hit by an automobile and left bruised and battered, a number of bones broken. In his agony he called out to God, "Why me? What have I done to deserve all of this?" He thought he heard a voice from heaven saying, "Sam, you haven't done anything wrong. There is just something about you that ticks me off."

Discouragement can make you believe that you've offended God. Is that true? Of course not. God doesn't act in that kind of capricious manner. How do I know that? Because the Bible is clear on the subject.

When you were a teenager did you go to one of those Christian camps where there was a closing campfire? If you did, you'll remember how you took a pine cone or a stick, which represented your sin, and you threw it in the fire. If you were like me, you then told God that from that point on you were going to be obedient and different. You were going to be God's person.

Those are good experiences, and I don't want to say anything against them. But you can easily make promises of obedience sitting by a campfire in the mountains, with all your friends singing hymns about Jesus. When you come back home and your mother wants you to carry out the garbage, though, the promises aren't so easy to keep. It took me a long time to recognize that feelings are changeable and a decision made on the basis of feelings, even a good one, probably would change.

There is, of course, nothing wrong with decisions based on feelings except that those kinds of decisions hardly ever last unless they are reinforced with facts. If you are encouraged by certain feelings, you will be discouraged by others. If you are encouraged by facts, no matter how discouraged you become, the facts won't change.

Someone has said, "Never doubt in the dark what God has taught you in the light." That's good advice. Some of my friends find great comfort in prayer and studying the Scriptures when they are going through a difficult time, but that isn't the way it works for me. When my rope breaks, the Scriptures seem as dry as dust and my prayers never seem to get any further than my front teeth. I study the Scriptures and pray when things are going reasonably well. Then, when the darkness comes, I remember the truth I discovered in the light, and I hang on to that with everything I've got.

In your dealing with discouragement, knowing Bible doctrine is essential because it gives you eternal truths, facts that are constant in spite of what your feelings are at any particular moment. Sometimes I don't feel like a Christian; sometimes I feel that God could not possibly be a God of love; sometimes I feel that there could not possibly be any meaning in my broken rope; sometimes I feel that God has cast me aside and that my life has been wasted. But, you see, feelings are just that— feelings. They have no reality of their own. That is why I remember in the dark the truth that I learned in the light.

3. Remember the Process

Third, when your rope is broken and you are discouraged, don't forget that God works out His purpose in the process. The psalmist wrote:

> *The steps of a good man are ordered by the LORD,*
> *And He delights in his way.*

Though he fall, he shall not be utterly cast down;
For the LORD upholds him with His hand."
                                        Ps. 37:23-24

Let me tell you a secret. When you're up, you think you'll never be down, and when you're down, you think you'll never be up. But in the process of living you will go through times of success and joy and times of failure and discouragement.

In New England folks have a saying about the weather: If you don't like it, just wait a couple of minutes and it will change. Discouragement is like that. It comes and it goes, so you need not assume that a state of discouragement, or encouragement for that matter, is permanent. When God decides that your broken rope has accomplished its purpose, He will fix the rope, and the discouragement will be fixed too.

My brother, Ron, spent a summer with us on Cape Cod to make some money to pay for his college education. He started out as a waiter because someone had told him that, with the big tips, he would make as much as two or three thousand dollars. That job lasted about two days. After numerous botched orders, broken plates, and angry customers, both Ron and his employer decided that Ron was not cut out to be a waiter. He then got a construction job. The construction contract ran out and he was laid off.

He came into my study one day and said, "Brother, this whole summer was a mistake. I should have stayed at home." I tried to encourage him, but in fact, I agreed with him. The summer hadn't turned out the way either one of us had expected. But when I got home for dinner that evening, Ron was in a much better mood. I figured that he had found another job, but that wasn't the case.

"Steve," he told me, "I got to thinking this afternoon and decided that my life could change in the next five minutes. Why get discouraged?" He was right. The next day he got a job as a ranger on a golf course, and it was one of the best summer jobs he ever had.

Ron understood something we all ought to remember: the only thing that doesn't change is the fact that change happens. Remember, every day the world rolls over on top of someone who was just sitting on top of it.

Let me repeat one of my favorite axioms: You can stand almost anything if you know it isn't permanent. As a pastor, I am constantly amazed at the resilience of God's people. The worst tragedy bringing the most terrible depression eventually dissipates through the power of God's grace. It doesn't always fade quickly or easily, but it does fade away. Just accept your discouragement now as a part of God's purpose, and be still until the light of understanding and grace shines.

4. Look to the Future

Finally, when your rope has broken and you are discouraged, don't forget the future. Paul wrote about what we can look forward to as believers:

Behold, I tell you a mystery: We shall not all sleep, but we shall all be changed—in a moment, in the twinkling of an eye, at the last trumpet. For the trumpet will sound, and the dead will be raised incorruptible, and we shall be changed. For this corruptible must put on incorruption, and this mortal must put on immortality . . . . then shall be brought to pass the saying that is written: "Death is swallowed up in victory."

1 Cor. 15:51–54

Richard Wurmbrand, who has dealt often with broken ropes, is a voice of hope in the midst of discouragement. He spent some fourteen years in communist prisons and is an example of a follower of Christ who, with hope and love, survived the worst that one man could do to another.

Wurmbrand, discussing the atheism of communism, spoke of the hope we have for the future. He suggested that if someone were to speak to an embryo, he or she might say that there was a wonderful life beyond the womb. If the embryo should answer the way an atheist would, it would say, "Don't bother me with this kind of religious superstition. This is my world, and it's the only one I know. I cannot see beyond it, and it is pure opiate to suggest that there is anything beyond."

"But suppose," Wurmbrand wrote,

this embryo could think with greater discernment than our academicians. It would say to itself: "Eyes develop in my head. To what purpose? There is nothing to see. Legs grow. I do not even have room to stretch them. Why should they grow? And why do arms and hands grow? I have to keep them folded over my breast. They embarrass me and my mother. My whole development in the womb is senseless unless there follows a life with light and colour and many objects for my eyes to see. The place in which I'll spend this other life must be large and varied. I will have to run in it. Therefore my legs grow. It will be a life of work and struggle. Therefore I grow arms and fists, which are of no use here."[2]

Broken ropes and the accompanying discouragement remind us that this life isn't the way it ought to be. Thirst may not prove there is water, and hunger may not

137

prove there is food. But thirst and hunger are very good indicators that there is something somewhere to fulfill those needs, something for resolution and completion, pointing to the future and to a promise.

"Let not your heart be troubled; you believe in God, believe also in Me. In My Father's house are many mansions; if it were not so, I would have told you. I go to prepare a place for you" (John 14:1-2).

When your rope is broken and you are discouraged, remember the memorials God has given you in the past and look to the future with the confidence that He has prepared a place for you.

9

Principalities, Powers, and Rulers of the Dark

A. W. Tozer wrote:

> Show me an individual or a congregation committed to spiritual progress with the Lord, interested in what the Bible teaches about spiritual perfection and victory, and I will show you where there is strong and immediate de fiance by the devil! Satan has been in this business of intimidating and silencing and oppressing the people of God for a long, long time.[1]

Someone else put it this way: "If you didn't meet the Devil this morning it is a good indication that you were going in the same direction."

Could It Be . . . Satan?

There are many times when broken ropes are the result of sin. Job's friends' explanations gave some validity for the problem of his suffering. Their explanations, however, were wrong. Although the friends' philosophical and theological views were quite insightful and biblical, they missed the real cause of his misery and suffering.

How do I know they were wrong? I know because I have an advantage over Job and his friends. I've read the

first part of the book. In the first chapter Satan came before God, and the Lord asked if he had seen that there
was no one on earth like His servant Job, "a blameless
and upright man."

> *So Satan answered the* LORD *and said, "Does Job fear God for
> nothing? Have You not made a hedge around him, around his
> household, and around all that he has on every side? You have
> blessed the work of his hands, and his possessions have in-
> creased in the land. But now, stretch out Your hand and touch
> all that he has, and he will surely curse You to Your face!" So
> the* LORD *said to Satan, "Behold, all that he has is in your
> power; only do not lay a hand on his person." Then Satan went
> out from the presence of the* LORD."
>
> *Job 1:9–12*

If you have read the story, you know that Satan went
after everything important to Job. He took away Job's
family, fortune, and reputation. Through it all, Job remained faithful to God. Thus Satan went back to God so
he might inflict more pain on Job (see Job 2:3–7).

I want to show you five important facts about broken ropes as they apply to Satan and his minions.

Alive and Well

The first thing you ought to notice about Satan is
that he is alive and well. Many of you have been reading
this book and have agreed with a lot of it up to this point.
But right now, you're saying, "Steve, you've got to be
kidding. Satan? That's a cop out. You preachers are all
the same. When you can't explain something, you blame
it on the devil."

Because I knew some of you would be saying that or
something like it, I thought about leaving this chapter

out. But the more I thought about it, the more I realized that a discussion of broken ropes without a discussion of Satan would be like discussing World War II without discussing Adolf Hitler.

The writers of the Bible called Satan the liar, the accuser, the dragon, the serpent, and the ruler of the world. The Bible says enough about the work of Satan to make any believer pause. Satan is the tempter, who would lure the believer away from the walk of faith. He seeks to destroy God's Word in the experience of the believer. He is an accuser, who would cripple the Christian with guilt and fear. He sometimes becomes regnant in an individual's life.

Satan is responsible for sin and unbelief, and he rejoices whenever he can turn a pagan away from Christ and a Christian away from the Christian life. He would have you fall down and worship him even if you called him by another name. He is real; he is alive; he is dangerous.

Some of the clearest teaching we have on this being of absolute evil comes from the lips of Jesus Himself. If Jesus was the Son of God as He said He was, then everything He said was true and only a very foolish Christian would ignore it. What, then, did Jesus say about Satan? When Jesus saw the unbelief of many so-called religious people, He said,

> *"Why do you not understand My speech? Because you are not able to listen to My word. You are of your father the devil, and the desires of your father you want to do. He was a murderer from the beginning, and does not stand in the truth, because there is no truth in him. When he speaks a lie, he speaks from his own resources, for he is a liar and the father of it."*
> *John 8:43–44*

141

Jesus pointed to Satan as the reason the truth of God does not take root: "The sower sows the word. And these are the ones by the wayside where the word is sown. And when they hear, Satan comes immediately and takes away the word that was sown in their hearts" (Mark 4:14–15). Jesus called Satan the "ruler of this world" (John 12:31). And Jesus predicted Peter's denial with these words:

> *"Simon, Simon! Indeed, Satan has asked for you, that he may sift you as wheat. But I have prayed for you, that your faith should not fail; and when you have returned to Me, strengthen your brethren."*
>
> Lk. 22:31–32

Now, you may still have difficulty believing in a real and personal devil. If that is your situation, don't skip this chapter. Just substitute the words *metaphorical personification of evil* every time you see the word *Satan* or *devil*. Your designation, I believe, will be wrong, but the ammunition will be effective nevertheless.

Under God's Control

Second, not only do we learn from Job that Satan is alive and well, but we also learn that Satan is controlled. An English proverb says, "The Devil is God's ape." Please note that before Satan could do anything to Job, he asked God's permission. Satan, though alive and well, is a defeated enemy (see Col. 2:15; Rev. 20:10). The Christian is playing in a ball game that has already been decided. The victory has already been won. Satan will come out on the short end of the stick! You can count on it because on the cross of Christ, God won the battle over Satan.

Cases of demon possession (yes, it actually does happen) are far fewer in modern industrial countries than in underdeveloped countries. At least, that has been true until recently. As technology and science have increased people have relied less and less on the supernatural to solve problems. And, whereas God's power is not limited by belief, Satan's is. You see, Satan operates on fear, superstition, and credulity. In those societies where Satan is pictured as a rather weak and funny little man with a pitchfork, a tail, and a weird red suit, his power gets crippled.

Now, with the failure of science and technology to repair broken ropes, people in developed countries have gained an amazing interest and desire to participate in the occult. And with that interest and participation, there has been an amazing increase in the power of Satan.

Merrill Unger wrote,

The scope and power of modern occultism staggers the imagination. Millions are unwittingly oppressed and enslaved by the occult. No wonder mental and emotional problems increase at an alarming rate. Unless the reality and purpose of Satan and demons are acknowledged, some of these problems will not be solved.[7]

Although Satan is alive and well and the activity of the occult has grown, Christians need to realize that Satan's power is limited and controlled by God. We must be careful not to give Satan credit for too many broken ropes. He already gets more credit than he deserves.

Early in my ministry a young man in the city where I was a pastor found out that he was dying of cancer. He was the father of a little boy and very respected in the community; however, he was not a Christian. Through the experience of cancer, he came to Christ, and his salvation became the most important thing in his life. In the months preceding his death I spent a lot of time with this young man, reading the Scriptures and praying with him. I believe that God can heal cancer and have seen Him do it. But God did not heal my new friend and brother.

Part of the "job description" of a pastor is to prepare people for death. I was preparing my friend for death when another Christian brother got the idea that my friend was dying of cancer because of satanic involvement. Without my permission, he visited my friend's hospital room just a few days before my friend died and told him, "God does not want you to have cancer. It is because of Satan that you have cancer." He went on to ask my friend if there had ever been any occult involvement in his family and discovered that my friend had once read a book on numerology. From that bit of "hard evidence" this man proceeded to perform a service of exorcism.

That was bad enough, but what was worse was the fact that my friend's parents, who were not Christians, attended the service. And when my friend's wife came later that evening, he blamed her for buying the book on numerology that caused him to cancer.

It took days to repair the damage in that particular case—damage done simply because someone attributed to Satan something Satan didn't do.

The point is this: Satan is God's lackey. If Satan has

anything to do with your broken rope, he has done only what a sovereign God has either allowed or ordained. Furthermore, any of Satan's works, no matter how horrible, can be the material with which God builds a monument of glory to Himself. Although it is important that we recognize the reality of Satan, it is even more important to realize that the Christian faith is not dualistic (i.e., there are not two opposite and equal powers, one good and one evil). The Bible proclaims that even Satan is part of God's economy.

The Student of God

Third, Satan is learning. God used Job as an instructive model for Satan. "Then the Lord said to Satan, 'Have you considered My servant Job'?" (Job 1:8). After Satan had done some horrible things to Job, Satan went into the presence of God once again, and God asked the same question: "'Have you considered My servant Job'?" (Job 2:3).

What does that mean? I don't know. But whatever it means, the Scriptures indicate that we are being viewed by supernatural beings that we might increase their knowledge and praise of God. Paul wrote to the Ephesians that grace was given, "to the intent that now the manifold wisdom of God might be made known by the church *to the principalities and powers in the heavenly places*" (Ephes. 3:10). Alfred Martin wrote that that verse gave "further indication that heavenly beings are observing the Church and seeing in the Church the unfolding of God's wisdom. Both good and evil angels are evidently amazed at the working of God as seen in redeemed men and women."[3] Your broken rope might have meaning far beyond the natural. It could be that you, like Job, are

145

serving as a model for Satan that he might be instructed in the power and glory of God.

I have been told that my witness was important. But nobody ever told me that my witness had an impact in "heavenly places." If God wants to use my broken rope as a model to Satan of the sufficiency of God's grace, I don't like it, but I will accept it.

In C. S. Lewis's book *The Screwtape Letters*, Screwtape, one of the head demons, writes to his nephew, Wormwood, advising and instructing him as to how he should conduct his demonic business with a particular individual:

> Do not be deceived, Wormwood. Our cause is never more in danger than when a human, no longer desiring, but still intending, to do our Enemy's will, looks round upon a universe from which every trace of Him seems to have vanished, and asks why he has been forsaken, and still obeys.[4]

We have seen before that Christians are not immune to broken ropes. I'm glad we aren't. If we were, pagans couldn't ever see the difference in us. God is interested in showing an unbelieving world the difference in the way Christians deal with suffering and hurt and fear. If He is interested in showing the same thing to Satan, I'm glad to be a part of his educational plan.

A Defeated Foe

Fourth, not only is Satan alive and well, controlled and learning, but Satan also is, for all intents and purposes, defeated. The Bible says, "Having disarmed principalities and powers, He [Jesus] made a public spectacle of them, triumphing over them" (Col. 2:15). Satan is dead; he just doesn't know it.

"So, if Satan is a defeated foe," you might ask, "why do I still have so much trouble with him?" The problem is appropriation. In other words, we have not internalized that which has already been done on our behalf. Suppose I had a very rich aunt who lived in another state and she died and left me a million dollars. Suppose further that I didn't know she had died and that I didn't know about my inheritance. I might be very poor because of my ignorance about the million dollars, but I would be very rich *in fact*. In order to turn my poverty into wealth, however, I would have to appropriate the money—that is, go to the bank and get it—for myself. Many Christians are ignorant of the victory over Satan that was won for them on the cross. Because of that ignorance, they have never appropriated it for themselves.

Have you ever visited the ghost house at Disney World or Disneyland? You are placed on a moving seat, and the seat takes you to places where, if you are like me, you don't really want to go. There is one scene where one can actually see ghost figures dancing in a living room. At another place you look in the mirror you're passing, and you see a ghost riding with you. In both of those places your heart may skip a beat, but you know the ghosts can't hurt you because they aren't real. They have been created by the amazing technology of the Disney people. As long as you remember that, you'll be fine. But if you somehow forget where you are or if you should start taking seriously what you are seeing, you are liable to die of a heart attack.

The Christian whose rope has been broken by Satan should remember who created Satan; remember who is in control of the world, including Satan; remember the One to whom you belong. If you remember that, you can say, "You can scare me, but you can't destroy me, because God rules you too. I will suffer, but I won't ultimately be defeated, because I can't be defeated by an enemy who is himself defeated. I will cling to my knowledge of the truth until the light shines."

A Silent Enemy

Finally, from the book of Job we learn that Satan is alive and sometimes not recognized. Satan hovered throughout the book of Job; however, he was never mentioned, acknowledged, or referred to throughout the rest of the book. In other words, he was doing some pretty horrible things and nobody knew that he was the one doing them.

That can happen when we are dealing with broken rope. Although I don't believe we should start looking for Satan under every bed and behind every corner, I do believe that we ought to be aware of his presence. The elders of the church I serve meet with me for prayer before each worship service. That time of prayer is one of the very special times of my week. All the elders kneel, and each prays for the service and the needs of the congregation. Almost always, one of the elders will pray, "And Father, we pray that Satan be bound and that our church and the worship service be protected and covered by the blood of Christ."

That prayer recognizes a reality—the reality of Satan, who would destroy all that God is doing. Recognition of his existence is the first step in dealing with him. Ultimately he can't destroy God's work. But even a weak enemy can hurt you if he sneaks up on you from behind.

Heinrich Heine, the nineteenth-century German poet, made a delightful reference to Satan in his "Pictures of Travels, The Return Home":

> I call'd the devil, and he came
> And with wonder his form did I closely scan;
> He is not ugly, and is not lame,
> But really a handsome and charming man.
>
> A man in the prime of life is the devil,
> Obliging, a man of the world, and civil;
> A diplomat too, well skill'd in debate
> He talks quite glibly of church and state.[5]

Our problem is that we think of Satan in certain traditional ways and look for him to appear that way. As a matter of fact, he hardly ever appears as we expect him to, and for that reason, we fail to recognize him. Have you ever thought that Satan was involved in the temptation that so assaulted you that you yielded and suffered from a broken rope? Have you ever seen his grin in the motivation of the friend who stabbed you in the back? Have you ever considered that Satan might even use a Christian brother or sister to hurt you?

Perhaps Satan was involved in those areas which led to your divorce. Have you ever looked for him in your depression? Have you found him lurking behind your broken heart? Have you thought of him as the author of discouragement? Satan is sometimes involved in all of that and more. Make sure that you learn to smell his presence. That is a part of the growing God is doing in your life.

Because Satan is often thought to be myth and because, in a sophisticated time, we don't believe in "wizards that peep and mutter," even Christians, when they have so many problems to confront, can easily decide that it is silly to think about something seemingly so remote as Satan. That is a terrible mistake. In his book *Faust Revisited: Some Thoughts on Satan*, Marshall W. Fishwick pointed to the problem of those who underestimate the power of Satan. He advised:

> No one who does go out should underestimate the task. Evil is active, eternal, omnipresent, contagious. We must expect to encounter it wherever we go, whatever we do. Satan never sleeps; he never even rests on his arms. When we think he is gone he is most there. When we are proudest we most readily betray ourselves.[6]

How Do You Handle the Enemy?

One question is still before us with regard to this subject: If Satan is involved in my broken rope, what can I do about it?

Learn to Use the Truth

When Paul spoke about how a Christian ought to resist Satan, he said that we are to have our loins girded with truth (see Ephes. 6:14). In that same passage he told us to take the sword of the Spirit, which is the Word of God (see Ephes. 6:17).

Use the Word of God to assess your situation, and apply it to your life. If someone tells me that my mother doesn't exist, how do you think I would answer that person? I certainly wouldn't compose a philosophical treatise on the subject of the existence of mothers in general and the existence of my mother in particular. I would simply affirm the fact that my existence presupposes the existence of my mother. I would offer a taste of my mother's banana pudding. I would explain about the birds and the bees. The Christian who knows the Word of God can deal with Satan's lies. Jesus said that Satan is the "father of lies."

If, in the midst of BRS, you feel that God has deserted you, affirm the truth of His love for you. If you think that you will be destroyed, affirm the truth that God has given you eternal life in His Son. If you start believing that God is punishing you, affirm the truth of your forgiveness in Christ. If you think that there is no hope, affirm the truth that God has already defeated Satan. Truth is a powerful weapon in the hands of a believer suffering from the trauma of a broken rope.

Learn to Resist Satan

Peter said in 1 Peter 5:9 that we are to resist Satan. James put it this way, "Therefore submit to God. Resist the devil and he will flee from you" (James 4:7). The worst thing you can do when encountering Satan is to give up. Stand up and spit in his eye. Tell him to go to hell where he belongs. You will be surprised how often he does just that.

Of course, resistance doesn't mean that you resist Satan in your own power. If you stand, God and all the powers of heaven will stand with you. It is sort of like the garage door opener in our house. We have a very heavy garage door and my wife, who is very little, had trouble opening it. We bought one of those electric garage door openers, and it is wonderful. All Anna has to do is to press the button on the device in her car, and the garage door opens. The door doesn't open because she has an effective prayer life; it opens because she presses the button. Her little effort brings to bear all of the electricity of the power company to open the garage door. It is the same way for the Christian. When you stand and resist, you find a power that you never knew existed.

Make Prayer Your Hidden Resource

God's hand is not shortened that He cannot save you (see Isa. 59:1). Because of Christ's death for you on the cross, you have been afforded the high and holy privilege of walking into the control room of the universe. You, because of Christ, can boldly approach the throne of God, who rules and sustains everything that is. You have been given the amazing privilege of going before a God who loves you, where you can plead your case. John Bunyan was right: "Pray often; for prayer is a shield for the soul, a sacrifice to God, and a scourge for Satan."

Martin Luther once said that we ought to be careful in our dealing with the devil because he had been around a long time and had a vast amount of experience. That truth scares me to death. At least, it does until I remember that I have a personal relationship with the One who has been around far longer than the devil and who has far more experience than he does.

Learn to Submit Everything

The other part of James's instruction for our dealings with Satan is submission to God. There comes a time when you sense satanic involvement in your broken rope. When you have done everything you can do in your dealings with Satan and the broken rope continues, what do you do then? You submit to God, knowing that He is in control of the situation and that Satan is being used by God for God's purposes. Submission to God is very difficult in those circumstances, but when you have done everything else, there is simply nothing left to do. Don't worry. You can trust Him. He hasn't made any mistakes so far, and I suspect He won't make any when you trust His plan for Satan's involvement in your broken rope.

A friend gave me the text of an order written by C. J. Auchinleck, the commander-in-chief of the Middle East Force during the Second World War:

> There exists a real danger that our friend Rommel is becoming a king or magician or bogey-man to our troops, who are talking far too much about him. He is by no means a superman, although he is undoubtedly very energetic and able. Even if he were a superman, it would still be highly undesirable that our men should credit him with supernatural powers.
>
> I wish you to dispel by all possible means the idea that Rommel represents something more than the ordinary. The more important thing now is to see that we do not always talk of Rommel when we mean the enemy in Libya. We must refer to "the Germans" or "the Axis powers" or "the enemy" and not always be harping.
>
> Please ensure that this order is put into immediate effect, and impress upon all commanders that, from a psychological point of view, it is a matter of the highest importance.

Let me suggest that this kind of order about Satan ought to be issued to every Christian. Satan has incredible public relations. He is blamed for everything from dry cows to cancer. But he isn't as powerful as his public releases would suggest. Only God has the kind of power Satan claims. Try to remember that. It helps.

10

Questions, Questions, Questions

Some Christians believe that the essence of the Christian faith is to accept what God has ordained and leave the questions for later. I suspect there is something to that belief. The problem is, however, that very few of us can simply accept pain and not ask why.

In an article in the *Wall Street Journal*, Carrie Dolan relayed the myth of Pele, the goddess of volcanic eruptions in Hawaii. According to the story, the goddess cursed anyone who took volcanic rocks from the island as souvenirs. Of course, there is nothing to the myth, but you couldn't prove it by some of the people who have sent their rocks back. Hawaii has received money, apologies, and rocks from people who felt that they had been cursed because they had taken souvenirs from one of the volcanoes. One man even blamed a bleak love life on the fact that he taken a piece of lava. He wrote, "Relay my sincere regrets to Pele. Undoubtedly, being a goddess and all, she knows who I am."

Wouldn't it be nice if we could attribute all our broken ropes to something as simple as our having stolen a few rocks? It wouldn't make any sense, but at least we wouldn't be perplexed with a lot of questions. We would have a simple answer to all our problems: We'd just return the rocks.

A Time for Questions

Unfortunately, our broken ropes don't lend themselves to easy questions or answers. In fact, one of the most terrible things about broken ropes is the perplexity involved. Questions are inseparable from broken ropes.

Are you familiar with John the Baptist? He was one of the great men of the Bible, ordained of God to be the forerunner of the Messiah, Jesus. He baptized Jesus and pointed to Him as the One about whom the prophets had spoken.

If you had known John the Baptist, you probably would not have liked him. Even if you *had* liked him, you probably wouldn't have introduced him to your friends. He was dressed in camel's hair clothing, he ate locusts and honey, and his language was just as earthy as his demeanor. He would not have been acceptable in most of our homes and certainly not in our churches. John's message from God shook the foundations of the religious and governmental establishment. He offended almost everyone except the common people, who flocked to hear his message of repentance.

John's problems began when he offended Herod. That offense couldn't be ignored: Herod was the king. Herod had John arrested in order to teach John a lesson. But one night the daughter of Herod's wife performed a strip show for Herod at a party. Herod was drunk and in that drunken stupor he promised his stepdaughter anything she wished. To Herod's horror, she requested the head of John the Baptist on a platter. The next morning Herod honored the girl's wish. After all, it would not be fitting for a king to fail to fulfill his public promises.

The eleventh chapter of Matthew records an interesting occurrence between the time John was in prison and the time he was executed:

> *And when John had heard in prison about the works of Christ, he sent two of his disciples and said to Him, "Are You the Coming One, or do we look for another?" Jesus answered and said to them, "Go and tell John the things which you hear and see: The blind receive their sight and the lame walk; the lepers are cleansed and the deaf hear; the dead are raised up and the poor have the gospel preached to them. And blessed is he who is not offended because of Me."*
>
> Matt. 11:2–6

Do you see it? John was in prison, and he knew he was going to die. His rope had broken, but he had been hanging on to one thing: the fact that he had been called by God to proclaim the coming of the Messiah. His faithfulness was giving him a certain degree of satisfaction. And then John had a passing and frightening thought: *What if Jesus is not the Messiah? What if I have missed the point of my entire life? What if I have blown this whole thing?*

You see, John had given up a lot for God. He had given up the comfort of family and friends, a wife and a home. He had given up the things that make life bearable. It hadn't been easy, but he had done it for God. Perhaps he had consoled himself with the thought, *God will bless me for my faithfulness. I have given up much, but God will balance the books.*

Suddenly one day, instead of receiving a blessing, John was thrown in prison and on the next day was scheduled to die. His rope had broken and the one thing he depended on looked as though it might come apart. Jesus had seemed to be the Messiah. He had fulfilled much prophecy. But Jesus had not become the reigning king predicted by many of the prophets. And that was what was worrying John. It was a time for questions.

Let's look at the different kinds of perplexity reflected by John and his disciples.

Intellectual Perplexity

John wanted to know intellectually whether or not Jesus was the Messiah. God has given us minds that are hard to turn off when the rope breaks. Aside from the hurt and the anguish, we ask honest, intellectual questions.

The questions reflecting our hurt are similar to the questions of John and his disciples. Is all of this we have believed really true? How could this happen from the hand of One who talked so much about love? If He cares for us so much, why do we hurt so badly? Sometimes the pain will blur the questions, but they are always there just under the surface.

While John the Baptist struggled with intellectual perplexity, his disciples endured emotional perplexity. They wanted to know if they should look for another Messiah. It was too late for John; he was going to die. But the disciples had invested emotionally in John and in what John believed. As they thought of the future, they were frightened. They needed a new cause.

Emotional Perplexity

Broken ropes create an emotional perplexity that corresponds directly to our emotional involvement in the situation. We not only face the pain of divorce but also the emotions that cascade through our minds as we consider the future and what will happen. We experience not only the tragedy of loss when a loved one dies but

157

also the fear of what will happen in the future without the one we love. Not only do we hurt over a child on drugs but we also fear what will happen as a result of the drugs. The emotional perplexity we feel is sometimes as great or greater than the reality of the broken rope itself.

A man was bankrupt. His business, which had started so well, had rapidly deteriorated, and now his lawyer said that the only thing left was to try to salvage something from the bankruptcy court. He had defined himself, his worth, in terms of his business, and with that failure he didn't know if he could go on. His questions poured out: *Will I be able to start over again? What will people say about me now? Can I still face my friends? Where do I go from here?* His emotional perplexity hurt more than the loss of his business.

Existential Perplexity

You should also note the existential perplexity John the Baptist faced. Matthew says that when John heard about the works of Jesus he sent his disciples to ask questions. John was going *to die*, and he faced the possibility of having invested his life in a meaningless enterprise. He was losing all hope: death was imminent and he didn't have any power to stop it. So he began to ask questions.

The person facing a broken rope feels the pain alone. It is existential and real. Questions are to be expected: How can this be happening to me? I've been faithful, and now, instead of a reward, I'm going to be executed. How can a fair God allow something like this to happen?

One of the most horrible things about being a pastor is that I am often called upon to bring bad news to people who, until I arrive on the scene, are doing quite well. I remember telling a young man that his father had just committed suicide. He wanted to know how his father had done it, and I had to tell him. I've walked the long hallway to the waiting room, where I have had to tell the family that they need not hope anymore because their father just died. I've driven to the home in the middle of the night to bring the news of a boy killed in an automobile accident. The questions are sometimes so painful that I try not to hear them. *Why? Why? Why?*

Accepting the Questions

Jesus could have easily said to John's disciples, "I can't believe it! John the Baptist, the prophet, is questioning? He is frightened? You go tell him to pray about it. He needs to remember that he must be an example to others! He must not question, and if he must question, tell him to keep his questions to himself."

But that isn't what Jesus did. He said, "Go and tell John the things which you hear and see" (v. 4). Jesus wasn't surprised or shocked. He accepted John's perplexity as the most normal thing in the world. It was.

When you have a broken rope, do you ever doubt? Have questions? Wonder? Of course, you do. Do you ever feel guilty about your questions? Don't! Jesus accepts every one of them.

When Helen Hayes cooked her first turkey for Thanksgiving, she called her husband and son together and said, "Now I know this is the first turkey I've ever cooked. If it isn't right, I don't want anybody to say a word. We'll just get up from the table without comment, put on our hats and coats, and go down to the hotel for Thanksgiving dinner." She then went into the kitchen to

159

get the turkey. When she returned to the table, her husband and her son were standing there with their hats, gloves, and coats already on.

God never accepts that kind of doubt. But for the believer who doubts and questions there is always acceptance. If you have gone so far that you can't get out, and then you doubt, God will accept it from you. But He can't abide the silly, superficial questions of the man or woman who has no will to believe. You have to have eaten the turkey before you ask your questions.

Let me tell you something most people don't usually consider: Only a believer can doubt because only a believer has anything to doubt. A pagan's questions are mere intellectual games. A Christian who is suffering and questioning is comparing the reality of his or her broken rope with the reality of the God he or she has experienced and known. God accepts those kinds of questions.

Jesus said, "I am the truth" (John 14:6). If Jesus is the truth, then all questions are welcome. If you are studying mathematics and you question the teacher about the multiplication tables, the teacher is not going to get angry and reject you. The teacher is going to accept your questions and go back over the lesson. Why? Because she knows that the multiplication table is chiseled into the very nature of the universe.

In the same way, the questions we ask in the midst of our tragedy and failure are accepted, because the God we question knows the truth of our situation—indeed, He is the truth.

Affirming the Questioner

Go back and read all the great things Jesus said

about John. He said that he was a prophet, and then He said that John was even more than a prophet. Jesus pointed to prophecy about John the Baptist. He said that no one born of woman was greater than John.

We want to say: "Now wait just a moment. I can understand how You would accept the questions, but to say all of those things about John is simply a public relations blunder. Don't ever use someone as a model who is making a mess of it. Wait until John gets his act together. Then hold him up as an example of faithfulness and belief."

But that isn't what Jesus did. Jesus not only accepted but also affirmed John the Baptist. Have you noticed in the gospels how Jesus appealed to the prostitutes and the lowlifes? Was it because they needed Him more than the church folks did? No! He appealed to them because they knew they needed Him. The only requirement Jesus ever made for His presence and help was our honest, verbalized need. John was no exception.

Have you ever noticed that the most rebellious child in the family is often the most loved? I have a friend who has three children, two of whom have done quite well. One is a pastor, and the other has a good business. Those two have never given their parents a moment of trouble. The third, Jimmy, has been nothing but trouble. For almost two years Jimmy has not called home, and his parents have no idea where he is. I once asked my friend which child was his favorite. "Steve," he said, "that's a question I can't answer. I love them all." Then his eyes welled up with tears and he said, "But I love Jimmy so much and I miss him so."

Too often we think God won't love us if we bring our questions to Him, so we allow the questions about

161

our broken ropes to drive us away from Him. That was one of Job's problems. In the midst of his horror he had a great fear:

> *"Only two things do not do to me,*
> *Then I will not hide myself from You:*
> *Withdraw Your hand far from me,*
> *And let not the dread of You make me afraid."*
> *Job 13:20–21*

Jesus told a story about a man who invited his friends to a dinner party. All of the guests gave excuses as to why they couldn't come. "So that servant came and reported these things to his master. Then the master of the house, being angry, said to his servant, 'Go out quickly into the streets and lanes of the city, and bring in here the poor and the maimed and the lame and the blind'" (Lk. 14:21).

The story shows that Jesus is attracted to people you wouldn't expect. He loves those who struggle. The Christian who says in the midst of a broken rope situation, "I'm just praising the Lord. Everything is wonderful," is missing an opportunity to experience the great depths of God's unconditional love.

As we have seen, we live in a fallen world. Things are not wonderful. Christians who don't have questions about the hurt and the tragedy in this world are often shallow and superficial. I am comforted in knowing that when I bring my questions to Jesus He doesn't turn me away.

Answering the Questions

When John came to Jesus, Jesus answered his

questions—at least, almost all of the questions. Jesus didn't go into a long dissertation on the Incarnation. He didn't explain to John about eternal life and why it is a viable and rational doctrine. But Jesus did answer enough of the questions to comfort John. Jesus reminded John about the prophecies in Isaiah with regard to the Messiah's giving sight to the blind, making the lame walk, cleansing the lepers, making the deaf hear (see Isa. 29:18; 35:5-6; 61:1-3). Jesus said to John's disciples, "You go tell John what you have seen."

Jesus gave John enough answers to make John's broken rope bearable and He does that for us.

When I am facing a broken rope and I think I can no longer believe in a loving and caring God, Jesus sends some angels to me. He tells them, "You go tell Stephen. . . "

At one time I thought that anyone who believed in the Christian faith had to leave their mind on the doorstep. And then some friends opened the door of rational Christianity to me. I remember how surprised I was that intelligent people believed in Christ. I was shocked to discover that the Christian world view was the only one that made any intellectual sense. If I had listened then, I would have heard Jesus bend over to an angel sitting next to the throne and say, "You go tell Stephen. . . "

I remember when our daughter Jennifer became sick and the doctor gave me some very bad news. Devastated and unable to pray for myself, I asked some friends to pray. The doctor called the next morning, surprised: my daughter was going to be fine. Jesus must have told an angel, "You go tell Stephen . . . "

Last week I was having a "pity party," thinking that I just couldn't go on comforting people when my own

163

heart was so broken. In the midst of my depression I got a call from a friend in another state. "Steve," he said, "you have been much on my mind lately. I've been praying for you. Have I ever told you how your ministry has touched my life and changed it?" At that moment I heard Jesus say to an angel, "You go tell Stephen . . . "

If you will take the time to look carefully when your rope breaks, you will see that the broken rope is not the only reality. There is light at both ends of the tunnel. If you will remember the light, the times He has said yes to your prayers, the times when you have known His presence, the ways He has helped others through you in the past, the hurts He has healed, and the times He has bound up your broken heart, you will find enough encouragement to keep on keeping on.

As I was flying from Chicago to Miami recently, I sat next to one of the captains of the airline. He was flying to Miami and then on to South America. It was a great opportunity for me to settle some fears I had about planes. I introduced myself to the pilot, whose name was John, and told him he was an answer to my prayer. "I have a great deal of fear about flying, even though I spend a significant portion of my time on airplanes. I always have a lot of questions, and if you don't mind, since I believe you are an answer to prayer, I would like to ask you some questions during this flight." John gave me permission to ask.

Every time I would hear a noise I would interrupt John from his reading and ask, "John, what was that?" Then, he would explain the noise to me and go back to his reading. Again and again, I interrupted John with my questions and, I must say, he was very patient and gracious with me.

Once when the plane went through some turbulence, I interrupted him again and asked, "What was that?" He explained the problem, but I didn't understand. He tried again. Finally, seeing that I didn't understand his explanation, he said to me, "Steve, it is a little complicated. Since I probably can't explain it to you in a way you can understand, just trust me it is O. K." I did trust him and felt better about the flight. You see, he had demonstrated his competence, and, in the areas where I didn't understand and he couldn't explain, I was willing to trust his word.

A great number of your questions have been answered. So if some of your questions haven't been answered yet, take comfort in knowing that if God has the answers to some of your questions, He has the answers to the rest. When you get to heaven He will answer them all. Then you will understand fully, even as you have been fully understood (see 1 Cor. 13:12).

Michael Quoist's book *Prayers* includes a prayer I have found quite meaningful when I have questions. I suspect it is the kind of prayer John the Baptist prayed just before he sent his disciples to Jesus.

Lord, it is dark.
Lord, are you here in my darkness?
Your light has gone out, and so has its reflection on
    men and on all the things around me.
Everything seems grey and somber as when a fog
    blots out the sun and enshrouds the earth.
Everything is an effort, everything is difficult, and I
    am heavyfooted and slow.
Every morning I am overwhelmed at the thought of
    another day.
I long for an end, I yearn for the oblivion of death.

165

I should like to leave,
Run away,
Flee,
Anywhere, escape.
Escape what?
You, Lord, others, myself, I don't know,
But leave,
Flee.

I go along haltingly, like a drunkard,
From force of habit, unconsciously.
I go through the same motions each day, but I know
that they are meaningless.
I walk, but I know that I am getting nowhere.
I speak, and my words seem dreadfully empty, for
they can reach only human ears and not the living
souls who are far above.
Ideas themselves escape me, and I find it hard to
think.
I stammer, confused, blushing,
And I feel ridiculous
And abashed, for people will notice me.
Lord, am I losing my mind?
Or is all this what you want?

It wouldn't matter, except that I am alone.
I am alone.
You have taken me far, Lord; trusting, I followed you,
and you walked at my side,
And now, in the middle of the desert, at night,
suddenly you have disappeared.
I call, and you do not answer.
I search, and I do not find you.
I have left everything, and now am left alone.
Your absence is my suffering.

Lord, it is dark.

Lord, are you here in my darkness?
Where are you, Lord?
Do you love me still?
Or have I wearied you?
Lord, answer,
Answer!

It is dark.[1]

It does get dark when your rope breaks. But in the dark you see the light better. Jesus said, "I am the light" (John 8:12). When it got dark enough, when the questions got so heavy that he had to ask, when the perplexity was eating away at his faith, John went to Jesus. He saw enough light to die with hope. And when John got home, there was no darkness.

11

Does My Father Know I'm Hurt?

I'm glad to reach this last chapter. Perhaps you are too. The pages of this book have been difficult for me in the same way a funeral is difficult. When you attend a funeral you have to face the unpleasant reality of your own mortality. While writing these pages, I have had to relive some of my own broken ropes and face the possibility of other broken ropes in the future. Some people have the misconception that writers and teachers provide help to deal with problems but don't need help themselves. No matter how much I would wish it otherwise, I can not speak of the human race as an outsider. I have broken ropes as anyone else does.

I suspect that my feelings are similar to Judith Viorst's feelings when she wrote her book, *Necessary Losses:*

> Somewhat wrinkled, highly vulnerable and non-negotiably mortal, I have been examining losses. These we confront when we are confronted by the inescapable fact . . .
>
> that our mother is going to leave us, and we will leave her;
>
> that our mother's love can never be ours alone;
>
> that what hurts us cannot always be kissed and made better;

that we are essentially out here on our own;

that we will have to accept—in other people and ourselves—the mingling of love with hate, of the good with the bad;

that no matter how wise and beautiful and charming a girl may be, she still cannot grow up to marry her dad;

that our options are constricted by anatomy and guilt;

that there are flaws in every human connection;

that our status on this planet is implacably impermanent;

and that we are utterly powerless to offer ourselves or those we love protection—protection from danger and pain, from the inroads of time, from the coming of age, from the coming of death; protection from our necessary losses.[1]

I wonder if most of the people who are in the helping professions are there because they need help. One often hears stories abut physicians who went into medicine because either they or someone they loved suffered. I have friends who are psychiatrists and psychologists because they have suffered emotional traumas. Chuck Colson developed a great burden for prisons because he had been in prison.

When John Newton converted to Christianity after having worked as a slave trader, no one was more surprised than John. At the church in London where Newton was the pastor, an epitaph remains, which John Newton wrote for himself: "Sacred to the memory of John Newton, once a libertine and blasphemer and slave of slaves in Africa, but renewed, purified, pardoned, and appointed to preach that Gospel which he had laboured to destroy."

I love the colorful way Newton described his conversion: "Once I was a wild thing off the coast of Africa. But Jesus Christ caught me and tamed me, and now people come to see me as they come to see the wild animals in the zoo."

When he was dying, Newton was visited by a young pastor who stood in awe of the dying man's contribution to the Kingdom of God. He expressed to Newton his deep feelings of regret and loss at Newton's impending death. Newton said to him, "True. I'm going on before you, but you'll soon come after me. When you arrive, our friendship will no doubt cause you to inquire for me. But I can tell you already where you'll most likely find me—I'll be sitting at the feet of the thief whom Jesus saved in His dying moments on the cross."

Wounded healers are the only kind God uses to do His work. As I have written these pages, I have dealt with my own hurts. Sometimes my doubts have haunted me in the middle of the night. At other times I have questioned whether one so human, so sinful, so afraid should be writing a book like this. There have been times when this book itself has become a broken rope.

I have dealt with the demon of discouragement and thought, *God, just leave me alone. I never asked for any of this. Let somebody else write the books and preach the sermons.* During these last months I have often identified with Francis Thompson:

> I fled Him, down the nights and down the days;
> I fled Him, down the arches of the years;

I fled Him, down the labyrinthine ways
  Of my own mind; and in the mist of tears
I hid from Him, and under running laughter.
    Up vistaed slopes, I sped;
    And shot, precipitated,
Adown Titanic glooms of chasmed fears,
From those strong Feet that followed, followed after.
    But with unhurrying chase,
    And unperturbed pace,
  Deliberate speed, majestic instancy,
    They beat, —and a Voice beat
    More instant than the Feet:
"All things betray thee, who betrayest Me."[2]

Now that I am almost through, I'm glad I have written the book. You see, the Watcher of broken ropes has been with me during the entire time of my writing. When I have written about discouragement or bitterness or guilt or Satan, I have felt God's presence. As I have relived my struggles, I have relived the memory of His faithfulness. As I have shared with Him my doubts, I have encountered His strength and love. As I have lifted my pain before Him, He has accepted it and reminded me of His own.

I have thought about the broken ropes of the people I love in the congregation I serve, and I have received God's assurance that God is deeply concerned by and intimately involved with "their story." I have thought about the helplessness I feel as a pastor when I am dealing with broken ropes, and the Father has reminded me that He cares more for those people than I do—and I care a lot. As the days and weeks have passed and the pages of this book have accumulated, I have sensed God's presence in a way that only those who have dealt with broken ropes can know.

The Father Knows

That brings me to the main point of this chapter and, I must say, the main point of the whole book. A sovereign God allows broken ropes because of His love. Our wondering if the Father knows about His people's hurt is similar to our wondering if the Father knew or cared about the hurt and suffering of Jesus on the cross.

If you are a parent, you have experienced the helplessness of watching your children hurt and knowing that you can't do a thing about it. But if you could choose to give your child a life of ease and bliss, if you could remove all obstacles and all pain, if you could smooth the road in a way that your child would never have a broken heart, never experience a sleepless night, never know failure, would you do it? Of course not. You know that the only way your child will grow into maturity is through the storms he or she will inevitably experience. You might soften the storm; you might make the wind a little less; you might ease the devastation; but you would never remove the storm. The storms have caused you to grow and change and mature. And in the deepest place of your heart you know that storms will do the same for your children.

It is amazing that a man could struggle and become successful and great, then use his success to shield his children from the struggles that made him great. Thinking parents know that the struggles are the stuff of which strength is made. God, of course, knows that too.

The Place of Broken Ropes

There is a place of broken ropes. It is not a pleasant place to visit, but everyone must go there at one time or another. If you are still, you can hear the sound of tears there as they strike the ground. Some people have been at the place of broken ropes so long they have set up residence. For many it is only a temporary place of darkness between the light which shines on both ends. Others didn't have to visit at all, but they came with someone they loved to share their sorrow.

The place of broken ropes will not always exist. It is only temporary, created by God's love. When it has served its purpose, God will erase it from human experience. But, for now, its grim specter haunts the dreams of those who have never even been there. "Someday," they say, "I, too, will have to visit the place of broken ropes."

There is a strange silence at the place of broken ropes. Almost all of the glib, silly explanations for its existence seem just that—glib and silly.

Vance Havner wrote:

> I get a little weary of these dear souls who have all the dealing and doing of Providence catalogued and correlated and figured out and can give you glib little answers to your heartache. They haven't been far. God just doesn't operate on our time table. And some of His operations don't add up on our computers. The little boy who didn't understand why God put so many vitamins in spinach and didn't put more of them in ice cream had a pretty good idea that it just doesn't work out like you'd think.[3]

The silence you find at the place of broken ropes is

not only the silence of those who reside there but also the silence of the Creator. Perhaps He is silent because He knows that the residents wouldn't understand His answers to their questions. Maybe the silence is a part of the broken rope, and even the silence of the Creator fits into His purpose.

Almost everyone at the place of broken ropes can identify with Job's cry:

> *But I would speak to the Almighty,*
> *And I desire to reason with God.*
> . . . .
> *Then call, and I will answer;*
> *Or let me speak, then You respond to me.*
> *How many are my iniquities and sins?*
> *Make me know my transgression and my sin.*
> *Why do You hide Your face,*
> *And regard me as Your enemy?*
> *Job 13:3, 22–24*

Have you ever felt that way? I have, and maybe that's the hardest part about visiting the place of broken ropes—experiencing the silence of God. Of course, we have questions about His silence: If He loves me, why does He remain silent? Why doesn't He tell me why I have to go through all of this? If I knew a reason, I could bear it. What do I have to do to get Him to speak? Have I offended Him? Does my broken rope indicate how He feels about me? And then we wait for answers, but all we can hear is the sound of our questions, bouncing off the walls of our emptiness.

Meeting God in the Silence

It is hard to bear the silence of God. But in that

place, and sometimes only in that place, you meet God. You may meet Him on the other side of silence, but you do meet Him.

I visited a man today who had jumped from the fifth floor of a hospital. The fifth floor was the psychiatric ward. He was so depressed that he didn't see any reason to live. So he jumped. He's going to live, and for now, he's safe. He has so many broken bones and open wounds that he can't make it to the window. He can't hold a pill or a knife or a gun, so he just lies there. They say it will take him at least a year to get well.

Someone had been reading one of my books to him and asked if he would like to talk to me. Today was my second visit, and today he was honest. He poured out his anger at God. "I tried," he said, the tears streaming down his face, "I tried to know God. I talked to Him, and He never answered." The silence of God, he indicated to me, was the reason for his despair. "I never can get Him when I need Him."

But now all he can do is be still. And because very few people visit because they don't know what to say, he will have to be silent. I told him that he would finally meet God in the silence. He didn't believe me, but he will.

Do you know how a shepherd trains a disobedient or wandering sheep? The shepherd breaks the sheep's leg, and then, while the leg is healing, the shepherd lovingly carries the sheep on his shoulders. The sheep who could never before find the Shepherd, finds nothing but the Shepherd during the healing of the broken rope.

I have a friend who will not meet with me unless we meet in a bar. I asked him once, "Why don't we get together sometime?" He told me that he always met his

175

friends in bars. If I wanted to meet him, that would have to be the place. He figured that he had gotten rid of the preacher . . . until I showed up in the bar. We have been meeting there ever since.

I could have manipulated him and got him to meet me somewhere else. I could have told him about the importance of a pastor's reputation. I could have complained about the booze and suggested that a bar was not an appropriate place to carry on a serious discussion. I could have told him that my study was quieter and more comfortable. But I didn't say those things. He would listen to what I said better, I decided, if I met him at a bar.

God meets us in places we don't expect. Because this is a fallen world, He meets us at the place where we all must live at one time or another, the place of broken ropes. Perhaps you are there now. At first, there will be silence, but in the silence He will speak. He won't answer all your questions; He's not a magician; He won't follow your agenda. But when you are finally quiet enough, He will come to meet you and the place of broken ropes will seem different because He came.

Do you remember how God came to Job? Job's suffering was almost unbearable. He questioned and cried and pouted and complained. Most of us would have done even more. The only response he got from God, however, was silence. But when everything had been said, when Job and his friends had used every cliché, when Job was spent and all was silent, God came.

Job's response to the God who came to the place of broken ropes was interesting:

"I know that You can do everything,

And that no purpose of Yours can be withheld from You.
You asked, 'Who is this who hides counsel without
knowledge?'
Therefore I have uttered what I did not understand,
Things too wonderful for me, which I did not know.
. . . .

I have heard of You by the hearing of the ear,
But now my eye sees You.

Job 42:2–3; 5

If you want to meet the living God, you almost always have to go to the place of broken ropes. After the silence, you will meet Him. And to meet God sometimes (if we were wiser, always) makes your visit to the place of broken ropes worth all the pain and suffering and hurt.

The Wounded Healer

When you meet God at the place of broken ropes, you will notice something else you didn't expect. God holds some broken ropes too. You will notice nail scars in His hands. You will see pain in His eyes, and you will know that the reason He speaks with authority is because the place of broken ropes is His place too.

Peter wrote, "Therefore, since Christ suffered for us in the flesh, arm yourselves also with the same mind" (1 Pet. 4:1). The writer of Hebrews said, "Though He was a Son, yet He learned obedience by the things which He suffered" (Heb. 5:8). "For we do not have a High Priest who cannot sympathize with our weaknesses, but was in all points tempted as we are, yet without sin" (Heb. 4:15).

A lot of the people at the place of broken ropes don't have to be there. They came because someone they loved

177

was there and they wanted to help. Some of those who came to help didn't stay very long. They found that the idea of helping and the act of helping are two different things. Those who left early had come from their place of security and peace. They condescended to come and help. Their motives were right and they didn't leave early because their love was lacking, or because their resolve was small, or because their compassion was inferior. They left early because their help was hollow and their words were empty. They would have stayed but they just couldn't understand; and because they couldn't understand, they couldn't help.

In the book of Job, Eliphaz's second speech was rather harsh. Job responded angrily:

> *"I have heard many such things;*
> *Miserable comforters are you all!*
> *Shall words of wind have an end?*
> *Or what provokes you that you answer?*
> *I also could speak as you do,*
> *If your soul were in my soul's place.*
> *I could heap up words against you,*
> *And shake my head at you;*
> *But I would strengthen you with my mouth,*
> *And the comfort of my lips would relieve your grief."*
> *Job 16:2–5*

Job was right. If the situation were reversed, he would have acted differently—but only because his rope had broken. After Job was sensitized to pain, he knew how to comfort.

That brings me to a principle: The best place (maybe the only place) to learn how to deal with someone else's hurt is to be hurt yourself. Alcoholics Anonymous has understood this principle, and that is the key to their effectiveness. They know that it takes an alcoholic to reach an alcoholic. The principle is built into the very nature of the universe and was lived out in the supreme model of truth: In the Incarnation, God came and experienced insurmountable hurt so He could visit the place of broken ropes and touch those who are there.

You are lonely and misunderstood. He, too, was lonely and misunderstood. You have failed. From man's standpoint, He failed too. You are afraid. He was afraid too. You have suffered the rejection of those you love. He, too, suffered the rejection of people He loved. Has someone you loved died? He lost people He loved too. You have to die. He died too.

Some people go to the place of broken ropes and are surprised to find Jesus there. After all, He is God. And then you think you understand. He is there to help all of us who have to come there. He is going to comfort you. That's what God is supposed to do, isn't it? But then you look more closely, and you discover that there are tears in His eyes. You see the scars on his hands and feet. And then you remember: He isn't there just to comfort; He is there because He belongs there.

The Order of the Broken Rope

You will discover that people who go to the place of broken ropes become part of a secret society called the Order of the Broken Rope. You never even know about it until you are a part of it, but the fellowship at the place of broken ropes is one of the good things about your being there. A broken rope will make you sensitive to others who have broken ropes. The apostle Peter encouraged suffering fellow believers to remain "steadfast in the faith, knowing that the same sufferings are experienced by your brotherhood in the world" (1 Pet. 5:9).

When my brother died, I thought I simply couldn't stand it. I thought that maybe no one had ever suffered as much as I was suffering. But I started getting cards and letters. "Steve, I understand and I will be praying. I lost my brother last year and I know what you are going through." A lady wrote, "My child was killed in an automobile accident over two years ago. It was horrible and it still hurts. God was faithful to us and he will be faithful to you." "Pastor, I wanted you to know that our family is praying for you. But we aren't praying that the hurt will be taken away. When our son died last year, the hurt was bad but God used it in our lives in a significant way."

I could go on and on. I discovered something through my brother's death: a fellowship of suffering. It is sometimes a very high price to pay to get into the Order of the Broken Rope, but you will meet people there with whom you will share something deep and important. You won't have to talk much. Sometimes a look, or a touch, or a smile, or a tear will identify you with the others. And when you recognize fellow sufferers, you will share and care in ways that only those who suffer understand.

When you go to the place of broken ropes you will find not only fellowship but also a subtle but real separation. Most people first arriving at the place of broken ropes congregate with others who have recently arrived. But gradually, two groups begin to emerge. They still understand and care about each other, but there is a difference.

Jesus described the two groups with a story of two

men. As in the story, both groups experienced a storm, but their responses differed:

"Whoever comes to Me, and hears My sayings and does them, I will show you whom he is like: He is like a man building a house, who dug deep and laid the foundation on the rock. And when the flood arose, the stream beat vehemently against that house, and could not shake it, for it was founded on the rock. But he who heard and did nothing is like a man who built a house on the earth without a foundation, against which the stream beat vehemently; and immediately it fell. And the ruin of that house was great."

Lk. 6:47–49

In C. S. Lewis's *The Great Divorce,* the souls of the departed dead meet in heaven. A mother whose son had died on earth met a bright spirit who had been the woman's brother, Reginald. Reginald explained to his sister some of the important facts of heaven and how she could get there. The woman simply couldn't see beyond the loss of her son in order to accept heaven and what it would take to see her son. Reginald went on to explain that her love for her son was wrong, and she replied, "Oh, of course, I'm wrong. Everything I say or do is wrong according to you."

"But of couse!" said the Spirit, shining with love and mirth so that my eyes were dazzled. "That's what we all find when we reach this country. We've all been wrong! That's the great joke. There's no need to go on pretending one was right! After that we begin living."

"How dare you laugh about it? Give me my boy. Do you hear? I don't care about all your rules and regula-

181

tions. I don't believe in a God who keeps mother and son apart. I believe in a God of Love. No one has a right to come between me and my son. Not even God. Tell Him that to His face. I want my boy, and I mean to have him. He is mine, do you understand? Mine, mine, mine, forever and ever.[4]

In the place of broken ropes you will either be drawn to God or you will walk farther and farther from Him. The broken ropes don't cause either. As in Jesus' parable, you will find whether your house is built on rock or sand. And broken ropes reveal the true condition of your relationship to God. And you will notice separation between the group drawn to God and the group walking away.

There is one final thing I want you to know about the place of broken ropes. At that place you will find hope. It is a hesitant hope. Sometimes it is hard to find in the midst of the tears and the pain, but it is there.

Listen to the words of Job in the midst of his despair, his friends' making fun of him and assuming that he has done something terribly evil even though he hasn't:

> *"For I know that my Redeemer lives,*
> *And He shall stand at last on the earth;*
> *And after my skin is destroyed, this I know,*
> *That in my flesh I shall see God,*
> *Whom I shall see for myself,*
> *And my eyes shall behold, and not another.*
> *How my heart yearns within me!"*
> *Job 19:25–27*

That is a surprise. You simply don't expect to find

hope in such a bleak place. But there it is, and I don't want you to miss it.

When Leighton and Jeanie Ford lost their son, Sandy, many of us suffered with these dear servants of God. Leighton wrote a book titled *Sandy, A Heart for God,* in which he related one of the "conversations" he had with Sandy:

> During the months following Sandy's death, to cope with my grief and sense of loss, I kept a journal. Through a series of "conversations" with Sandy, I continued to express my grief and bring our relationship to a close.
>
> In one of those chats, I said, "Sandy, you've been dead two months earthtime."
>
> "I feel as if I have been alive forever, Dad. It's a lot like one big long today."
>
> "It's a matter of time, Sandy, except that time heals. It's more a matter of nearness. I guess I'm concerned that as our time goes on, we will lose any sense of nearness."
>
> "But why, Dad? You're moving closer to eternity every day. You're no longer moving from, but to me! And besides, the 'Wall' between is so thin—you would laugh if you could see it."
>
> "I think more of you than when you were at Chapel Hill."
>
> "Sure! I know you do. I hear those thoughts."
>
> " 'Night, Son! Enjoy the stars!"
>
> "It's morning here, Dad. Enjoy the light!"[5]

It is no fun to go to the place of broken ropes. But the Creator of the place has promised that it won't always exist. When your hope is based in the promise of the Creator of broken ropes, you can count on the hope becoming a reality.

We can't cover up the reality of broken ropes. The Bible presents the unpleasant fact of broken ropes. Hebrews 11:13 says, "These all died in faith, not having received the promises" (v. 13). Now that is honest. But there is more—the hope of heaven and the light to come. You will always find the "more" at the place of broken ropes.

Be still. Listen to the hope: "Therefore God is not ashamed to be called their God, for He has prepared a city for them" (Heb. 11:16).

Recommended Reading

If you are interested in a larger discussion of the reasons for pain and suffering in the world, I suggest the following books.

Steve Brown, *If God Is in Charge*, Nashville: Thomas Nelson, 1983. (I will stoop to almost any level to sell books.)

C. S. Lewis, *The Problem of Pain*, New York: Macmillan, 1940.

Edith Schaeffer, *Affliction*, Old Tappan, New Jersey: Revell, 1978.

Philip Yancey, *Where Is God When It Hurts*, Grand Rapids: Zondervan, 1977.

There is no dearth of literature on the subject of evil and why it happens. One book I would not recommend for its faithfulness to Scripture is Rabbi Kushner's *When Bad Things Happen to Good People* (New York: Avon, 1981). Rabbi Kushner takes the classic question, If there is an all-loving and all-powerful God, why is there so much bad in the world? and says, in effect, that God is all-loving but He isn't all-powerful. The Bible teaches clearly that God is both all-loving and all-powerful. I would, however, recommend that book as an example of a compassionate and loving treatment of the subject by a man who has paid his dues and who is struggling with the issue.

NOTES

Chapter 3

1. Geoffrey Barloe, ed., *Vintage Muggeridge* (Grand Rapids, MI: Eerdmans, 1985), 115–116.
2. Isobel Kuhn, *Green Leaf in Drought Time* (Chicago: Moody Press, 1957), 7.

Chapter 5

1. Jean-Paul Sartre, "The Flies" in *No Exit and Three Other Plays* (New York: Vantage Books, 1955), 122.
2. J. R. R. Tolkien, *The Lord of the Rings*, Vol. III (Boston: Houghton Mifflin, 1983), 220–221.
3. Homer, *The Iliad and The Odyssey*, trans. Samuel Butler (Chicago: William Benton, 1952), 252.

Chapter 6

1. Chuck Colson, "My Cancer and the Good Health Hospital," *Christianity Today*. April 3, 1987, 56.

Chapter 7

1. David John Seel, *Does My Father Know I'm Hurt?* (Wheaton, IL: Tyndale House Publishers, 1971), 36.

2. Emily Dickinson, untitled poem in Jones, Leisy and Ludwig, eds., *Major American Writers* (New York: Harcourt, Brace, 1952), 1174.

3. C. S. Lewis, *Letters to an American Lady* (Grand Rapids, MI: Eerdmans, 1967), 8.

Chapter 8

1. Charles H. Spurgeon, *Lectures to My Students* (London: Marshall, Morgan & Scott, 1969), 161–162.

2. Richard Wurmbrand, *My Answer to the Moscow Atheists* (New Rochelle: Arlington House, 1975), 156–157.

Chapter 9

1. A. W. Tozer, *I Talk Back to the Devil* (Harrisburg, PA: Christian Publications, 1972), 10.

2. Merrill F. Unger, *Demons in the World Today* (Wheaton, IL: Tyndale House, 1971), 18.

3. Pfeiffer & Harrison, eds., *The Wycliffe Bible Commentary* (Chicago: Moody Press, 1962), 1308.

4. C. S. Lewis, *The Screwtape Letters* (New York: Macmillan, 1961), 39.

5. Heinrich Heine, "Pictures of Travels, The Return Home."

6. Marshall W. Fishwick, *Faust Revisited: Some Thoughts on Satan* (New York: The Seabury Press, 1963), 27.

Chapter 10

Michael Quoist, *Prayers* (New York: Sheed and Ward, 1963), 139–140.

Chapter 11

1. Judith Viorst, *Necessary Losses* (New York: Fawcett Gold Medal, 1986), 2–3.

2. Francis Thompson, "I Fled Him," in Lieder, Lovett & Root, eds., *British Poetry and Prose* (Boston: Houghton Mifflin, 1950), Vol. II, 801.

3. Vance Havner, "Reflections," *Christianity Today*. November 1986, 45.

4. C. S. Lewis, *The Great Divorce* (New York: Macmillian, 1952), 172–173.

5. Leighton Ford, *Sandy, A Heart for God* (Downers Grove: InterVarsity Press, 1985), 171.

Steve Brown is heard daily on Key Life radio network. He also appears, with Tony Campolo, on *Hashing It Out*, a TV program on the Faith and Values Channel. Steve was a pastor for many years before becoming professor of preaching at Reformed Theological Seminary. He is the author of many books.